MW00716087

Nurturing *the* Spiritual Growth *of* Today's Adolescent

In Your Home, School, & Parish

MICHAEL CAROTTA, EdD

Harcourt Religion Publishers

www.harcourtreligion.com

Copyright © 2002, 2007 Edition, by Harcourt Religion Publishers, a division of Harcourt, Inc.

All rights reserved. No part of this publication may be reproduced or transmitted in any form or by any means, electronic or mechanical, including photocopy, recording, or any information storage and retrieval system, without permission in writing from the publisher.

Requests for permission to make copies of any part of this work should be mailed to Permissions Department, Harcourt, Inc., 6277 Sea Harbor Drive, Orlando, Florida 32887-6777.

Printed in the United States of America

ISBN 0-15-902137-5

10 9 8 7 6 5 4 3 2 1

This book is dedicated to all parents and guardians who fiercely hold on to high hopes and healthy dreams for the spiritual life of their teens. It is also dedicated to those faithful and conscientious parents and guardians who have experienced the heartache of having good kids make bad decisions.

May the grace of God be with us all.

Contents

Chapter 4

Chapter 5

Chapter 6

Chapter 7

Introduction
Yesterday and Today

As a parent or guardian of an adolescent, you have no doubt noticed that the parenting techniques that worked for a first grader, or even a fifth grader, just don't work anymore.

Yesterday you ate together as a family. Today you're lucky if you can get to the drive-thru in time to get your teen to his or her music or sports practice. Yesterday your child asked questions. Today your teen has all the answers. Yesterday your child worked with you. Today your teen fights with you. Yesterday your child would run to your bedroom to escape nightmares. Today your teen's dreams keep him or her awake at night. Yesterday you wondered about your child's future. Today you worry about it. Yesterday your child was your baby. Today that child is your teen.

The differences between parenting a child and parenting an adolescent are not at all bad. In fact, the difference can be energizing, exciting, and rich. Today the conversations can matter in a deeper way. Today your authenticity is valued more than ever. And today you can play a significant role in helping your teen pursue his or her dreams, his or her promise to become.

Perhaps the most important difference between childhood and adolescence is the presence of passion. Whether you recognize it or not, your teen is filled with passion—passion that is much different from his or her energy as a child. This passion is more complex. It is what fuels his or her life.

Too often, we mistake *passion* to mean *lust*. But passion can also describe the determination it takes to practice a sport or musical instrument for hours every day. And it can mean moving non-stop on the dance floor, drooling over an awesome car, yelling during a school pep rally, or primping in front of a mirror until every hair is perfectly in place. Passion can represent the time and attention your teen gives to his or her friendships. It is passion that does somersaults in the yard and turns up the radio and sings along perfectly when a favorite song comes on. It is passion that cries tears of frustration, anger, or loss. And it is passion that moves adolescents to search for the deeper meaning, ask spiritual questions, and step toward the God who made them.

Don't stifle this passion. It is, after all, the gift adolescents bring to us. In fact, you have the opportunity to support and strengthen that passion with principles. Having passion and principles is like having a full tank of gas and a map. Passion with principles leads to *com*passion. Jesus taught (and taught with) compassion, and the Skills for Christian Living presented in this book can help you reinforce that same spirit in your teen and in yourself.

This book is intended to give you a better understanding of your teen and to help each of you recognize and develop the skills necessary to live out your callings as Christians. Chapter 1 introduces you to the world of your adolescent. While you may remember your own adolescence, your teen is growing up in quite a different world. Chapter 1 also explains the spirituality and specific needs of your adolescent. Finally, the chapter introduces you to the specific Skills for Christian Living that you will be using in Chapters 2 through 6. Each of these chapters contains a set of skills directed toward a special area—Religious Experience, Moral Decision Making, Emotional Management, Gospel Living, and Forecasting.

Chapter 7 offers concrete, faith-filled practices and ways to promote Catholic identity and put these skills into practice. It offers a tool for individuals and families to assess how they are already living out their faith, and how they can better do so.

Each skill will first be explained for you in a way that you can share with your teen. You'll then have a chance to apply the skill to your own spirituality before receiving specific and practical ways to reinforce that particular skill with your teen. You already know the importance of today in your teen's life and in your own. That is why this is not a book you read, but a book you do. Thanks for your willingness to work with it.

Chapter ❶

Early
Adolescents
Today

Adolescence in the New Millennium

The Needs of Adolescents

The Spirituality of Adolescents

Skills for Christian Living

Adolescence in the New Millennium

During a conference several years ago with 250 youth-serving professionals, Dr. David Elkind, author of The Hurried Child *and* All Grown Up and No Place to Go, *was asked how he would define "at-risk" youth. Most in the field at that time agreed that at-risk youth were those who were experiencing two of the following five dynamics: school failure, poverty, severe family conflict, criminal activity, and substance abuse. Dr. Elkind looked at the professional who asked the question with some confusion and then said firmly, "All early adolescents."*

What's unique about this list: e-mail, cable TV, the Internet, callwaiting, MTV, WWF, wine coolers, tattoos, global warming, metal detectors in public schools, beepers, cell phones, body piercing, high-priced athletic shoes, latch-key kids, AIDS, and CD and DVD players.

Answer: All the above items were part of your son's or daughter's childhood, while most of the items were not part of yours. Today's young adolescents experience new types of stresses every day, such as criminal activity, environmental concerns, purchasing power, substance abuse, academic and athletic pressures, and victimization.

We do not yet know the impact of these childhood experiences. But you as a parent or guardian can and should be clear about this: **You were never their age.** Like your adolescent, you were once twelve years old. But not *their* twelve. You were once fourteen. But not *their* fourteen. They have had an unprecedented childhood.

In his book, *In Over Our Heads: The Mental Demands of Modern Life* (Harvard University Press, 1994), Robert Kegan suggests another important fact—no one was ever *your* age either. Your parents were stressed, but in quite different ways. So here is a generation of youth who have experienced an unprecedented childhood, being parented by people who are in over their heads in an unprecedented experience of adulthood.

Let's uncover one more reality about adolescents today. When you were growing up, your society and your parents gave you markers, or signs, that showed you were leaving childhood and moving into the new and exciting world of adolescence. For example, you had to be a certain age before you could go somewhere unchaperoned. Whatever the markers were for you, they signaled your arrival into the time of life you were told you had to wait for—adolescence.

Today traditional markers are being accessed by children of younger ages, creating two major problems. First, young adolescents have not yet developed the verbal skills, cognitive ability, or life experience to navigate this frenzied and complex journey. We're asking children to grow up before they're ready, which is like asking them to bake a cake when they don't have all the ingredients. Second, older adolescents, seeing that young adolescents buy what they buy, wear what they wear, know what they know, listen to what they listen to, go where they go, and do what they do, conclude that there is really not much difference between twelve and sixteen. So what do older adolescents do? They leave traditional adolescence prematurely in search of adult markers of entertainment, relationships, employment, intoxication, independence, and so on. This puts them at risk as well. Both younger adolescents and older adolescents are now thrust into this culture of early access that they are not physically, mentally, emotionally, morally, or spiritually prepared to handle. This is why Elkind defined an entire generation as "at-risk."

So what can you as a parent or guardian do? Some might suggest that you back up and give your teen more space. After all, you were never their age. But what would happen if you step forward—toward the adolescent—with an intrusive presence that is neither obtrusive nor abusive. The ideal intrusive presence is one in which you are always knocking on the door of your teen's life, inquiring about the state of things, willing to listen to the absurdity of things, pointing out the important things, challenging the unhealthy things, celebrating the special things, clarifying the confusing things, insisting on the moral things, and rooting for the precious things.

For the purpose of this book, we use the word *teen* instead of *child* when referring to your young person for two reasons: First, we are working on the assumption that "early adolescence" or "younger adolescents" spans the 12–15-year-old age group, while "adolescence" or "older adolescents" refers to 15–18-year-olds. There is much debate today about such distinctions. Some experts refer to 10–15-year-olds as early adolescents and 8–12-year-olds as "tweeners" because they are in-between childhood and early adolescence.

Others consider young people up to and including age 21 to be adolescents. Using the word *teen* reflects the fact that experts do agree that young people are considered to be in some stage of adolescence before becoming thir*teen*.

Second, you can consider your young person to be distinctively different from how she or he was as a child in the intermediate grades without debating the onset or length of adolescence. Whether in the sixth grade or the ninth, your young person is emotionally, intellectually, socially, and spiritually different from how he or she was as a child. In this sense, your young person can be considered a *teen*.

There are skills that can help your teen develop a spirituality that enables him or her to cope better with the challenges of adolescence and contribute to the good of others. There are skills that can help your teen recognize God's presence and enrich her or his prayer life. There are skills that can help your teen grow as a person of character and conscience.

Therefore, this is not the kind of book you read. It is the kind of book you *do*. By *doing* this book, you will increase your confidence and competence to embrace the religious, emotional, and moral dimensions of your teen's development. Take your time as you work through this book. Find a comfortable place to sit, and just *do* one skill at a time.

The Needs of Adolescents

Check off the activities that your teen enjoys the most:

○ Playing sports
○ Playing video games
○ Shopping
○ Going to a dance
○ Buying new clothes
○ Religious events
○ Holidays
○ Family gatherings
○ Talking on the phone
○ School work
○ Surfing the Internet
○ Listening to music
○ Going to the movies
○ Going out with friends
○ Writing poetry or stories
○ Reading

○ Sleeping in
○ Eating out
○ Hanging around an older or younger sibling
○ Keeping a diary
○ Journaling
○ Collecting cards or other items
○ Organizing things
○ Watching TV
○ Being around members of the other gender
○ Joining a drama group
○ Helping you or another adult with projects
○ Being creative or artistic

We know that today's generation of young people has a high sense of social concerns and a high acceptance of diversity. Young people born in the 1990s embrace technology to a degree that astonishes many of their elders.

Experts tell us that the development of adolescents centers on meeting eight different needs.

Physical activity: Adolescents need physical activity in order to maintain a healthy balance of energy.

Self-definition: Your teen constantly needs to figure out who he or she is. He or she sorts out answers to such questions as, "What do I really like?" "What do I really hate doing?" "What am I good at?" "What kind of personality do I have, or want to have?" and "What's really important to me?"

Then there are the countless "why" questions, such as, "Why am I afraid to . . .?" "Why do I always . . .?" and "Why do people treat me like I'm . . .?" Keep in mind that young adolescents have two things running through their heads as they define themselves—a personal fable and imaginary advisors. Your teen has developed a story about himself or herself over the years that helps him or her make sense of the world. This personal fable tends to include elements that greatly exaggerate the adolescent's abilities or shortcomings. Sometimes the personal fable borders on invincibility or inferiority. Your teen's imaginary advisors consist of the people he or she thinks are always noticing, talking about, or supporting him or her.

Competence and achievement: Adolescents need to feel successful. Many want to be able to demonstrate concrete skills and talents. It helps them feel good about themselves.

Religious experience: Spiritual hunger is sometimes stronger in adolescence than in childhood simply because of what the adolescent is going through. Adolescents, for example, often experience a love/hate relationship with their friends. The adolescent experience of companionship, loyalty, and betrayal only makes the thought of God's unwavering presence *naturally* appealing. Your teen has certain thoughts that he or she is afraid to share with others for fear of rejection, judgment, or ridicule. The notion of a God who loves you unconditionally is *naturally* appealing to a young adolescent. Adolescence also includes an occasional and acute experience of powerlessness and anxiety. Once again, the notion that Jesus is a friend who is willing help with the tasks and challenges before him or her is *naturally* appealing to your teen.

Creative expression: Adolescents need to express themselves. In their minds they are thinking, "I've been a child all my life! Now I want to stand up and express myself." The problem is that adolescents often have not yet developed the verbal skills to say what's on their minds. This cognitive-linguistic gap between what they think and their ability to put these thoughts into words will lessen as they mature. But many of them are better able to express themselves through the clothes they wear; the music to which they listen; the activities for which they have a passion artwork, writings, posters; and the friends with whom they want to associate. Too often we expect adolescents to express themselves verbally—something a lot of them cannot do very well.

Positive interactions with peers and adults: When adolescents have good experiences with peers, it provides self-assurance that he or she is okay. You will begin to notice that your teen will silently hang around and mingle with your adult company when you have friends over. He or she won't say more than a word to two, but you'll notice that he or she lingers longer with the adults than ever before. Why? Because when your teen hangs around adults and seems to get along with them, it provides self-assurance that he or she is growing up.

Meaningful participation: Adolescents want to have input. They want to participate meaningfully in the direction of their lives. They want to control some of the decision making. So your teen will insist on wearing a T-shirt in the middle of winter or wearing those blue pants even though he or she asked your opinion and both of you agreed that the khaki ones looked better. They want their opinions included in conversations, and they want input into decisions. Adolescents also want to participate meaningfully in the lives of others. They want to do community service, but they don't have the organizational skills to pull it off without some adult direction. They will often reject "busy work" but will relish meaningful participation.

Structure and limits: Adolescents want to succeed. They need structure from adults in order to do well. Have you ever noticed how young adolescents are sticklers for the details whenever they are given instructions about a task? That's because they really want to do the task successfully. Adolescents also want limits. Even though they keep trying to renegotiate and test the limits, they find security in knowing that if they live within the limits they will be safe. To not give them limits is to increase the chaos of their early adolescence.

Here are three important exercises for you.

1. *Go back and find the activities you checked at the beginning of this section. Choose one activity and see if you can name any of the* *eight developmental needs of adolescents (EDNA) your teen is meeting through that activity.*

Activity:

Needs being met:

Looking at adolescents through the lenses of these eight developmental needs can help explain some of the negative behavior. Imagine that an adolescent gets caught stealing a CD from the music store. When asked why he or she did it, the young person responds, "I dunno." The truth is, the adolescent might really have no clue as to the reason for his or her negative behavior. However, EDNA may hold some clues. In an upside-down, inappropriate way, stealing the CD involved *positive interaction* from some peers who would be impressed with the youth's shoplifting success, a certain amount of *competence* and *achievement* in pulling off the caper without getting caught, *creative expression, physical activity,* and *meaningful participation.*

2. *Select one of the following negative behaviors. Can you name the developmental needs being met inappropriately? Try to identify at least four needs.*

- Premarital sex
- Drinking wine coolers at a party
- Being in a gang
- Sneaking into an R-rated movie with friends
- Telling parents or guardians that he or she is at a friend's house, when he or she has really gone to a party

Negative activity:

Needs being met:

3. One final note about these developmental needs: *Always show adolescents how inappropriate behavior actually hurts certain developmental needs.* After one or two illustrations, your teen can do this sort of analysis by himself or herself. *Try it yourself by going back to the negative behavior you selected above and listing the developmental needs that are impaired by that behavior.*

Negative activity:

Needs being interfered with:

The Spirituality of Adolescents

"God is in heaven; I'm here on earth. I pray every night to God above. God and I are tight. I talk to God at unplanned times, like waiting for the bus in the morning or standing in the front row before an awesome concert. I attend church often; I ask questions in religion class and really care a lot about maintaining my personal relationship with God."

Jason

"I believe in God and stuff. Like, I believe God is watching over me, but I don't pray much or go to church. My spirituality calls me to be a good listener, a faithful friend. My spirituality calls me to treat others fairly, to stick up for the person others make fun of. My spirituality calls me to accept others and not be prejudiced, to include those everyone else excludes, to care for those who are in need. . . ."

Christin

Adult family members often need advice about their teens who don't have any interest in religion, "you know, kids without any spirituality." But the question is not, "Do young people have spirituality?" The question is, "What kind of spirituality do young people have?"

Research continues to show us that adolescents do indeed have a spirituality: They believe in and experience God, pray often, believe in an afterlife, and acknowledge that God expects them to live a loving life. But it is important to remember that there is a difference between religion and spirituality. Religion involves denominational membership, participation in religious traditions, and understanding of religious teachings. Spirituality includes those with religious affiliation, while at the same time those who are not active members of any religious denomination.

When you think about the spirituality of your adolescent, think in terms of *direction,* or *dimension.* It is helpful to think of spirituality consisting of three different, yet related, directions—in a sense, a 3-D view of spirituality.

The three directions are **vertical** (relationship with God), **horizontal** (relationships with other people), and **internal** (emotional).

Adolescents with a highly vertical direction in their spirituality place most of their attention and energy on their individual relationship with God. That's the spirituality described by Jason in the example at the beginning of this section. In the extreme, people with vertical spirituality invest so much in their religious and personal relationship with God that they do not invest anything in how they treat other people. Gang members wear rosaries and religious medals and crosses around their necks as a sign of their deep personal relationship with God. At the same time, many live a life of violence.

Adolescents with a horizontal direction of spirituality emphasize the moral life. For these young people spirituality is mostly about treating other people with kindness and honesty. This is the spirituality described by Christin in the other example at the beginning of this section. An adolescent with a highly horizontal spirituality invests in caring relationships with others and in living the moral life. In the extreme, however, this sort of adolescent spirituality does not invest in the religious or vertical dimension.

Finally, there is the internal direction of spirituality. People with highly internal spirituality say things such as, "My spirituality helps me deal with the things that hurt me inside," "My spirituality helps me accept myself—with all my warts," "My spirituality helps me forgive myself," or "My spirituality challenges me to use my potential." This internal direction of spirituality centers on emotional management, which is good and much needed—especially among adolescents who have very little help in dealing with their emotions. Today, however, it seems that this internal direction of spirituality is the most popular of the three directions among North American adults. An adolescent with an internally directed spirituality was not quoted at the beginning of this section because adolescents, in general, do not have that kind of spirituality. Spirituality of this sort seems to be at the heart of many of the adult spirituality books that appear on the bestseller lists. Unfortunately, in the extreme, people with a highly internal direction of spirituality don't invest in helping others or in maintaining any religious practices or denominational affiliation.

The task for all parents and guardians is to *pay attention* to the spirituality of their children—to try to glimpse the dominant direction of their spirituality. Once done, you should affirm it and attempt to nurture the other less-developed directions or dimensions of their spirituality. If you cannot glimpse a dominant direction within your teen's spirituality, then intentionally nurture one dimension or direction for a time, taking care to address all three directions within due time.

Skills for Christian Living

In and of itself, self-esteem offers nothing more than a mirage for those who work with children. Like all mirages, it is both appealing and perilously deceptive, luring us away from more rewarding developmental objectives. While capturing the imagination of parents and educators in recent years, the mission of bolstering children's self-esteem has obscured the more promising and productive possibilities of childrearing. We would do better to help children acquire the skills, values, and virtues on which a positive sense of self is properly built.

Greater Expectations by William Damon (Free Press, 1995)

Five common *myths* about adolescents:
- They don't get along with their parents.
- They are trouble and are troubled.
- Their faith life is weak.
- They are all the same.
- Their self-esteem is low.

Chances are that none of these statements apply to your teen. The most recent data on teens tells us that nearly three out of four get along with their parents very well and seek parental advice in times of stress. Among adolescents, at-risk behaviors such as smoking, substance abuse, pregnancy, crime, and failure in school are lower than in previous decades.

According to a 2003 national study of youth and religion, approximately 80 percent of adolescents report that they believe in God, heaven, and hell; pray regularly; and talk about religion. Over 80 percent of Catholic adolescents report that their religious faith is somewhat, very much, or extremely important in shaping decisions they make in their daily lives. Only 2 out of 10 report that they consider God distant, and 7 out of 10 want to learn more about their faith.

While teens all long for independence, acceptance, and a later curfew, they are very diverse. Some adolescents of the exact same age have great verbal skills, while others have not yet learned how to express themselves. Some adolescents can think abstractly, others not yet. Some have developed social poise, and some have not. Some have a spirituality that is predominantly vertical, and others have a far more horizontal spirituality.

Only about 6 percent of adolescents consider themselves to have low self–esteem. The research on self-esteem has shown this for more than twenty-five years. Low self-esteem is not an issue for U.S. teens, nor has it ever been. However, adolescents do report being depressed at times. Some carve themselves, some starve themselves, and some anesthetize themselves. Why do they struggle with depression? We are not sure. We know from the research that it is not because of low self-esteem. Perhaps it is because of an increasing sense of hopelessness, a negative world view, a sense of powerlessness, or a crisis of the spirit. Instead of focusing on adolescent problems, we would do much better to focus on adolescent potential and empowering our teens to feel competent, capable, and faith-filled.

Maintaining Presence

Guiding your teen through the difficult stage of adolescence can be a challenging but rewarding experience. As you learn and practice the Skills for Christian Living presented in this book, remember that each of these skill sets require you to continue to be an important *presence* in your adolescent's life.

Praise your teen by being specific and generous. "Nice job" is not good enough. Be specific. Let your teen know *exactly* what he or she did that was praiseworthy. For example, "Ashley, you really handled that well. Instead of getting into a screaming match with your brother, you calmly let him know that what he did embarrassed you. I thought that was a very mature thing to do. Thanks."

Religious beliefs and experiences should be shared and explained. Even though your teen may not value your religious traditions or share your religious beliefs today, he or she wants to know why they are important to you. In fact, as your adolescent begins to make sense of his or her own religious experience, many of your traditions may become an important part of his or her spirituality. This is a core element of your legacy that will live on in your teen's memory.

Expect your teen to maintain strong, but realistic values. Regardless of his or her environment, be stubborn about the high expectations you set for your teen's moral character. Expectations for character are those that emphasize integrity, responsibility, honesty, kindness, trustworthiness, respect, caring, justice, and so on. More times than not, your teen will meet your high expectations for these behaviors.

Sensitivity is an important trait in parenting. First, parenting is often nothing more than common sense. So be sensitive to your instincts and act on them. Second, be sensitive to your adolescent's struggles. Admit that you may not understand all of what he or she is going through, but promise to be there to provide support and guidance.

Examples shape your teen more than you will ever know. It is true that you may be the only Bible your adolescent will ever read. Your teen will read your actions like a book. Through your responses to everyday situations—the way you handle a stranger, a relative, stress, anger, affection, and ambition—you will be an important teacher for your teen.

No is a word you must be strong enough to use. It can indicate that you are willing to be a clear moral voice: "No. I can't support that behavior." "No. I really do think your decision was wrong." Don't use it so often that it looses impact. But use it whenever you need to help your adolescent maintain his or her integrity and moral values.

Courage is required with the job you took on as a parent or guardian. You have to have the courage to give structure and set limits, despite your teen's resistance. As often as parents or guardians need to have the courage to set limits, they also need to have the courage to apologize when they have made a mistake. Adolescents don't forget when a parent makes a true apology.

Express your emotions and help your teen do the same. Whether the emotion is joy, anger, sadness, or pride, it is important to express yourself. If you wait too long to express yourself, the power of the moment is lost. When you express your emotions properly and in a timely manner, you lead by example. Your teen then recognizes that it is okay to express himself or herself.

Sometimes you will have to work very hard to encourage your teen to express his or her emotions. But if you begin the process while your teen is an early adolescent, it will become easier as he or she gets older. That is why this book introduces Skills for Christian Living. Skills are concrete and helpful. This approach assumes that young people have the desire and ability to actively work on their own development. Skills help adolescents feel competent and capable. These skills respond directly to the eight developmental needs of adolescents (EDNA).

This approach has been tested and measured. Youth who have been introduced to some of these skills report that they can see the difference in their lives. They report that these skills help them become spiritually and morally stronger; give them confidence in dealing with their emotions; and enable them to make good decisions, enjoy life, and have hope for the future.

Be ready to reinforce the skills you have worked through in this book whenever you are in the company of your teen. Nothing else is as important. As you practice these skills, don't be content with any *presence*. Instead, develop an intrusive presence in your teen's journey to adulthood. An intrusive presence does not mean using extreme actions that are obtrusive or abusive. Similarly, it means more than simply paying lip service to your role.

An intrusive presence means being a consistent and persistent presence in the world of your young adolescent. Remember that as you work with your teen, God's Spirit, who is life's greatest truth and its greatest mystery, will also be intrusive.

The following chapters will introduce you to skills in five different areas: Religious Experience, Moral Decision Making, Emotional Management, Gospel Living (or Justice and Service), and Forecasting.

Religious Experience skills help improve one's ability to communicate with God. They strengthen the *vertical*, or religious, dimension of spirituality. Such skills include:
- *How to Pray*
- *Recognizing God's Presence*
- *Keeping the Lord's Day*
- *Applying the Bible Message*
- *Using Religious Imagination*
- *Celebrating*

Moral Decision Making skills help improve one's ability to relate to one another. They strengthen the *horizontal* direction of spirituality and include:

- *Social Analysis*
- *Forming Conscience*
- *Being Accountable*
- *Examining Conscience*
- *Confronting*
- *Discerning What Is Right*

Emotional Management skills strengthen the *internal* dimension of spirituality by helping one deal with strong feelings that have a direct impact on one's moral life. Such skills include:

- *Staying Hopeful*
- *Handling Anger*
- *Lamenting*
- *Expressing Affection*
- *Dealing with Anxiety*
- *Letting Go*

Gospel Living skills touch on all three dimensions of spirituality and include:

- *Practicing Empathy*
- *Reconciling*
- *Giving Thanks*
- *Offering Solidarity*
- *Honoring the Body*
- *Resolving Conflicts*

Forecasting skills help one anticipate upcoming situations and take initiative for the next step. These skills help young people move out of a passive and reactionary mode and into a more active and productive mode. The skills touch on all three dimensions of spirituality and include:

- *Goal Setting*
- *Keeping Promises*
- *Identifying Consequences*
- *Choosing Good Friends*
- *Making Changes*
- *Reverencing the Ordinary*

Each skill will be dealt with in three parts. The first section introduces the skill, the second gives you the opportunity to practice the skill and assess your own abilities, and the third offers suggestions for reinforcing the skill with your teen. As you become familiar with these Skills for Christian Living, you can become more of a coach or mentor for your adolescent and, in the process, find practical ways to be an intrusive presence.

Chapter **2**

Religious
Experience

How to Pray

Recognizing God's Presence

Keeping the Lord's Day

Applying the Bible Message

Using Religious Imagination

Celebrating

*These skills are designed to help improve the
way we relate to and maintain a friendship
with God. These skills strengthen the vertical,
or religious, dimension of our spirituality.*

How to Pray

Likewise the Spirit helps us in our weakness; for we do not know how to pray as we ought, but that very Spirit intercedes with sighs too deep for words. And God, who searches the heart, knows what is the mind of the Spirit, because the Spirit intercedes for the saints according to the will of God.

Romans 8:26–27

Introducing the Skill

In prayer we raise our minds and hearts to God. There are many forms of prayer. The *Catechism of the Catholic Church* mentions the following forms: blessing and adoration of God, petition for our own needs (which includes asking for forgiveness), intercession for the needs of others, thanksgiving, and praise. We can express these forms of prayer in many different ways. Most often we use vocal prayer, meditation, or contemplative prayer, which is a prayer of silent union with God.

We educate our children on the need to pray and the benefits of praying, and we share our belief that God hears our prayers. We strive to build an appreciation for prayer within our children, hoping that they, too, can find prayer to be the most basic and most important tool for spiritual growth. But none of these efforts is the same as intentionally teaching young adolescents *how to pray*. In so teaching we need to move beyond the words of memorized prayer to engage our "minds and hearts," to speak to God from the depths of our spirits and to be open to the Lord's response.

There are many obstacles to prayer. Therefore, learning how to pray involves discipline.

List three obstacles to prayer you think your teen faces:

1.

2.

3.

One way to integrate some of the forms and expressions of prayer is to use the following model. Coach your teen to TAPP into God's presence during prayer by doing the following:

T hank and praise God for the good things you have been given and the good people in your life.

A dmit the things you may have done wrong or the opportunities to help others that you ignored.

P etition God for your needs and intercede for the needs of others. But remember that there is a difference between what you *want* and what you *need*.

P onder what God has to say to you. Practice pausing long enough to listen.

The four components of TAPP do not have to be done in any particular order. These four components are intended to provide a clear, direct, and well-balanced conversation with God. Work with your teen to develop other ways to pray. You may have already developed your own format or might consider doing so now.

For Yourself

1. What are your first memories of praying? Can you remember the *Where, When, How,* and *Who* of your earliest experience? Describe your memories.

2. How has your practice of prayer evolved since childhood?

3. What obstacles to prayer do you face?

4. Where is your favorite place to pray now?

5. The passage from Paul's Letter to the Romans at the beginning of the skill addresses the kind of prayer that uses no words. In this prayer you place yourself in the presence of God. However, there are many ways to pray. Check off any of the following that you already use to be aware that you are in God's presence. Place a star by any situations that you would like to develop as an experience of prayer.

- ○ Praying while listening to music
- ○ Praying while walking or jogging
- ○ Praying while bathing or showering
- ○ Praying while alone
- ○ Praying in church during Mass
- ○ Praying while eating
- ○ Praying while sitting in an airplane

- ○ Praying while gardening
- ○ Praying while reading a good book
- ○ Praying in the morning or evening when no one else is around
- ○ Praying while driving to work
- ○ Praying while watching a movie
- ○ Praying while enjoying your favorite sport or hobby

Which of the earlier-mentioned parts of prayer could improve your prayer life?

Using the Skill

1. Some ways in which your teen prays may surprise you. Many of these ways, however, are common. The following have actually been shared by adolescents:

- Praying while wearing headphones
- Praying while standing in the front row of a sensational concert
- Praying while waiting for the school bus every morning
- Praying in the bathroom
- Praying during a car ride

- Praying while completing the halftime marching band routine
- Praying before taking a test
- Praying while riding a bike
- Praying while walking to school
- Praying before participating in a sports activity

What does this tell you about the adolescent practice of prayer?

2. You may find it helpful to recognize your teen's practice of prayer. Take the following quiz by circling your best guess for each item. Then ask your teen to answer them.

My teen prefers

Vocal prayer   *Meditative prayer*

Memorized prayer   *Group prayer*   *Unsure*

He or she prays

Very rarely   *Once in a while*

Often   *Regularly*   *Unsure*

My teen is _____ **with his or her prayer life.**

Not satisfied   *Satisfied*   *Very satisfied*   *Unsure*

When my teen prays, he or she does more

Thanking   *Admitting*   *Pondering*

Petitioning and Interceding   *Unsure*

3. Participating in community worship, such as attending Mass, can be a point of contention with your teen. Recognize that how you participate and how your teen chooses to participate may look different. Be prepared to share with your teen how you participate in Mass and what this participation means to you.

4. Further suggestions to explore the skill of How to Pray:

- Share a favorite prayer memory from childhood with your teen.

- Pray for your teen, and let him or her know you are doing so.

- At times ask your teen to pray for you when you need extra support, such as a presentation at work or stressful week ahead.

- Ask your teen to bless a meal before eating.

- Create a prayer-time ritual as a family on a weekly or daily basis.

- Create a "prayer petition" space. Use sticky notes for the posting of prayers.

Recognizing God's Presence

> *God is love, and those who abide in love abide in God, and God abides in them.*
>
> 1 John 4:16

Introducing the Skill

Believing in God and knowing a lot about God is not the same thing as *recognizing God's presence.* Recognizing God's presence is not always easy because God tends to make his presence known to us in the quiet of our hearts. We have to make an effort to hear God's voice in a noisy world full of stress, multiple commitments, and information overload.

List 3–5 things or "noises" in your teen's world that might make it hard for him or her to recognize God's presence or hear God's voice:

1.

2.

3.

4.

5.

Despite all the noise in your teen's life, he or she is born with the innate spiritual ability to sense the presence of God. The *Catechism of the Catholic Church* tells us that "Created in God's image and called to know and love him, the person who seeks God discovers certain ways of coming to know him" (#31). The Catechism goes on to say that deep within our souls we can recognize God's presence in truth, beauty, and love.

To develop in our children the skill of Recognizing God's Presence, we must help them use their spiritual "ears to hear" and "eyes to see" God as they encounter moments of truth, beauty, and love.

For Yourself

Take a moment to assess your own spiritual "eyes to see" and "ears to hear" by checking the statements below that are "very true" about you:

○ I recognize God's presence daily.

○ I've had at least one strong and memorable experience of God's presence in my life.

○ I sometimes am aware of God's presence through my friends.

○ I find it easy to detect God's presence in nature.

○ I see beauty in the world around me.

1. Name a truth you've come to realize within daily events, humanity, or creation that has helped you recognize God's presence.

2. List two things of beauty that have helped you experience the presence of God.

3. Describe a loving act that showed you the presence of God.

4. Based on your answers to the items above, how would you describe the way you recognize God's presence?

5. Finally, what experience or moment of grace in which you recognized God's presence would you like to share with your teen?

Using the Skill

1. Sometimes we can also recognize the presence of God in the *absence* of truth, beauty, or love. Therefore, expect to have discussions with your teen regarding the presence of God in adverse situations, such as:

- Someone is hurt by a lie.
- Someone makes a bad decision based on false information or myths.
- Someone breaks or loses a thing of beauty.
- A thing of beauty is intentionally destroyed.
- He or she witnesses an unloving act.

2. Pay attention to any possession or souvenir that your teen quietly but resolutely considers to be "special." Chances are good that it is special because it is a reminder of a moment of grace in which your teen recognized the presence of God.

3. Begin paying attention any time your teen and his or her friends turn up the radio to better hear (or sing along with) a favorite song. Sometimes adolescents love a certain song because it speaks of a truth that their hearts recognize. Such truths may also have a dimension that nourishes their spirits.

4. Don't hesitate to casually *identify* moments of grace that you and your teen experience together. "That person was like an angel of God helping us work this out." "Do you see that? What a beautiful sight! How could anyone think the beauty of nature is an accident?" "We really had a great trip. Let's thank God for that."

5. Practice openly giving thanks to God for the many good things you experience. This will heighten your teen's awareness of the presence of God in everyday events.

Keeping the Lord's Day

Observe the sabbath day and keep it holy, as the LORD your God commanded you. Six days you shall labor and do all your work. But the seventh day is a sabbath to the LORD your God; you shall not do any work . . . .

Deuteronomy 5:12–14

Introducing the Skill

Check off why your teen and his or her friends have a hard time keeping the Lord's day—worshiping and resting (refreshing body, mind, and spirit).

- ○ "I can pray by myself."
- ○ "Church is boring."
- ○ "I don't think I have to go to Mass every Sunday."
- ○ "I'm too busy."
- ○ "I don't want to be seen with my family at Mass."
- ○ "I spend weekends with my other parent, and he or she doesn't go to Mass."
- ○ "I participate in sports on the weekends."
- ○ "I clean my room on Sundays."
- ○ "I save my homework for Sunday evenings."
- ○ "I always need to be doing something. I can't sit still."

As parents we find ourselves having to explain to our children the reasons we do or don't keep the Lord's day. Here's one good reason for keeping the Lord's day you can share with your teen: It allows you to see *who* you are and *whose* you are. Adolescence is a time of busy schedules, emotional roller-coaster rides, low-level chaos, and hot-and-cold relationships. Psychologists tell us that all of this tends to leave adolescents uncertain about the kind of persons they are and want to become. The experience of adolescence sometimes leads them to question religious practice—if only briefly.

The practice of Keeping the Lord's Day provides us with time for a much-needed reflective pause. It allows us to sort quietly through the demands and complexity of the past week in order to notice what kind of persons we are and to reestablish our core values and dreams. This reflection is done through prayerful conversation with God.

The skill of Keeping the Lord's Day involves intentionally making Sunday a time of worship and rest. If possible, we need to make it a day that is not "business as usual" for our families.

Take time for worship. Because we are social beings and Christianity is anchored in community, it's important for us to reconnect with our faith community and to celebrate the Eucharist as the primary event of the Lord's day. Activities that allow young adolescents to recognize and experience the presence of God in beauty, truth, and love also remind them about *whose* they are.

Take time for rest. This means taking time for rest and leisure in order to nourish our family ties, enjoy cultural and social events, and strengthen our relationship with God. Sunday can be a time to read or relax, engage in physical activities and hobbies, and reflect. In this way we can relocate our spiritual and emotional compass.

For Yourself

Reflect on your current practice of Keeping the Lord's Day.

1. Overall, how intentional are you about setting aside time for worship *and* time for rest? (circle one)

   Not intentional at all   Somewhat intentional   Intentional

2. What part of Keeping the Lord's Day is harder for you? (circle one)

   Rest   Worship

3. How can you make Sunday rest and leisure with your family a priority?

4. What sort of activities currently help you experience truth, beauty, or love?

Keeping the Lord's Day has a special power to remind us *who* we as productive adults are — that is, the kind of person we are, not the kinds of things we are accomplishing. And Keeping the Lord's Day reminds us *whose* we are: children of God, not employees of a company. These two reminders can help us regain or maintain perspective and restore our souls. List one new way you can enhance your current approach to Keeping the Lord's Day.

Using the Skill

1. Prepare to respond to the following comments from your teen. Be sure to remember the dual purpose of Keeping the Lord's Day (worship and rest) and the dual effects of Keeping the Lord's Day (reminds you of *who* you are and *whose* you are).

> *"I can't go to church on Sunday because my soccer team is in a tournament! I didn't schedule the game on Sunday, so please don't punish me for it."*

> *"I don't have time for family activities because I have a science project due."*

> *"I get more out of praying alone in my room than going to Mass."*

> *"I have no life! I have to baby-sit at noon. If I go to church with you, I have no time on Sunday for anything else. Every other day of the week I have to wake up at 6:30 A.M., jump out of bed, and hurry to get ready for school. Sunday is my only chance to sleep in."*

"I don't want to go with my family to visit relatives. I need some time for me."

"I want to go to the mall with my friends instead of out to eat with my family."

2. To better reinforce worship and rest with your teen, place a *W* or an *R* next to any of the following adolescent activities that appropriately fit one of these two purposes.

   _____ Reading the Bible   _____ Going to the movies

   _____ Playing video games   _____ Spending time with

   _____ Listening to or   family members

         making music   _____ Being with friends

   _____ Playing a sport   _____ Participating in

   _____ Doing homework   the Eucharist

   _____ Praying   _____ Hiking

   _____ Shopping

3. If you heard your teen say, "Sometimes when I go to Mass, I don't sing at all. I close my eyes and listen to everyone else sing. It's like letting myself be sung to," how would you describe the effect worship is having on him or her?

4. List the three most important things you can do to foster in your teen the skill of Keeping the Lord's Day.

Applying the Bible Message

> *"Your word is a lamp to my feet and a light to my path."*
>
> Psalm 119:105

Introducing the Skill

Ask yourself these questions:

1. What words from Scripture might be guiding my teen's decisions? (For example, "Love one another as I have loved you.")

2. What are the most meaningful stories from Scripture for my teen? (For example, the prodigal son.)

We can all learn what is in the Bible, how it came to be written, and the various literary forms within it. We can learn to appreciate the Bible as God's word, a source of direction, comfort, and moral decision making. But knowledge of, and appreciation for, the Bible is not the same thing as developing the skill of Applying the Bible Message *to our lives.* The Bible speaks to us about four different things:

Conscience—what is right and what is wrong

Character—the kind of people we are

Contribution—what we do to help others

Knowledge of God—the nature and characteristics of God

Any time you hear or read the word of God, ask yourself this question: Is God's word speaking to me about my conscience, character, contribution, or knowledge of God?

For Yourself

Try practicing the skill of Applying the Bible Message by describing how you see Conscience, Character, Contribution, or Knowledge of God in the following Scripture passages:

1. "It is good to give thanks to the LORD,
       to sing praises to your name, O Most High;
   to declare your steadfast love in the morning,
       and your faithfulness by night. . . ." *Psalm 92:1–2*

2. ". . . and if anyone forces you to go one mile, go also the second mile. Give to everyone who begs from you, and do not refuse anyone who wants to borrow from you." *Matthew 5:41–42*

3. "No one can serve two masters; for a slave will either hate the one and love the other, or be devoted to the one and despise the other. You cannot serve God and wealth." *Matthew 6:24*

4. "You have heard that it was said, 'You shall not commit adultery.' But I say to you that everyone who looks at a woman with lust has already committed adultery with her in his heart." *Matthew 5:27–28*

Take some time to think about the meaning of this Scripture passage in your life:

"Do not store up for yourselves treasures on earth, where moth and rust consume and where thieves break in and steal; but store up for yourselves treasures in heaven, where neither moth nor rust consumes and where thieves do not break in and steal. . . . For where your treasure is, there your heart will be also." *Matthew 6:19–21*

Using the Skill

1. While driving home from church, ask your teen: "Did the readings talk about Character, Conscience, Contribution, or the Knowledge of God?"

2. There are Catholic youth Bibles that include reflective questions and exercises to help adolescents think through the meaning of Scripture. Buy your teen a Bible for Christmas, Easter, or his or her birthday, and encourage him or her to use it.

3. At many sporting events, someone will hold up a yellow sign with a Scripture citation, such as *John 3:16,* written on it. With your teen, look up the reference and ask him or her to tell you what that Scripture passage means. Discuss why this is such an important message. (*John 3:16* is considered a summary of the gospel message.)

4. Plan ahead. Set up a time in which you and your teen can go over the quote at the beginning of this section and discuss the two questions. Form a Scripture study partnership once a week or once a month. Read a passage and designate a time to talk about it.

5. Target one of the following to work on *gradually* with your teen:
   • Read the Bible more often.
   • Develop a conviction that the Bible has a lot to say to him or her today.
   • Make the Bible an important source of moral direction.
   • Hold informal family discussions on applying various Bible messages.

Using Religious Imagination

"I am the true vine, and my Father is the vinegrower."

John 15:1

Introducing the Skill

This Scripture passage is just one of many examples of how Jesus taught in a way that encouraged us to use our religious imagination. All of us have religious imagination, including your teen. Religious imagination is like a muscle we are each born with, but we need to exercise it. When your teen exercises his or her religious imagination, several things happen: he or she makes sense of the spiritual aspects of life, experiences "God moments," and grows in his or her understanding of God through the abundant use of symbols and imagery in Catholicism.

A group of students were asked to describe one of their favorite Catholic symbols. One student said, "Incense." The leader assumed that the student appreciated the symbolism of the smoke of incense rising up to the sky as our prayers rise up to God but wanted to test the assumption. So the leader asked the student to explain why. The student replied, "Because it reminds me that you pray best after you get burned."

Using Religious Imagination is not a skill that is taught. It is a skill that adolescents already possess, but one that you need to help them exercise. The key to helping your teen use his or her religious imagination is to *honor the senses*. It seems that adolescents have a natural ability to *sense* the sacred. Plus they make *sense* out of things in ways adults don't.

There are four areas to explore when helping your teen exercise religious imagination:

- Catholic symbols and gestures
- Media (movies, music, television)
- Moments of grace
- Mystery

To help your teen use his or her religious imagination, wonder aloud sometime as to why the Advent wreath is a circle instead of a square, why we make the Sign of the Cross the way we do, why the priest wears green (or red or purple). Wonder aloud some time as to why people light candles in church or why people wear crosses around their necks.

Ask your teen to name his or her favorite Church holy day or season or why we don't just sit for the whole Mass, but also stand and kneel.

Ask your teen if he or she has ever felt as if an angel were with him or her or if he or she has an item that holds spiritual meaning. Ask if your teen has ever felt the presence of evil. Ask how your teen can tell if God is listening when he or she is praying. Ask him or her to tell you about a recent movie or song that had a spiritual message. Ask what your teen thinks God, or Jesus, really looks like.

For Yourself

1. What experience, conversation, movie, or moment engaged your religious imagination recently?

2. Which Catholic symbols or gestures engage your religious imagination? (Check all that apply.)

- O oil
- O holy water
- O wine
- O candles
- O altar
- O statues
- O crucifix
- O palms
- O chalice
- O religious medals
- O icons/paintings
- O stained glass windows
- O bread
- O Advent wreath
- O Easter Vigil fire
- O liturgical colors
- O carrying the Book of Readings in the entrance procession
- O making the Sign of the Cross
- O burning incense
- O saying "Amen"
- O kissing the cross on Good Friday
- O singing a hymn
- O splash of water during the sprinkling rite
- O Ash Wednesday ashes
- O a lit votive candle

3. The Paschal mystery refers to Jesus' suffering, death, and resurrection. It is rich imagery for a spirituality that embraces the cycles of life made up of trials, loss, and new beginnings. Practice exercising your religious imagination by making brief notes about how any of the following life experiences reflect the spirituality of the Paschal mystery.

You move your family to another state.

One of your parents develops Alzheimer's.

Your oldest child leaves for college.

Your teen gets cut from the school team.

A couple you love get a divorce.

You lose your job.

Other:

Using the Skill

1. Sometimes our culture uses religious language, symbols, and gestures—often in marketing new products. Discuss how religious imagination is sometimes misused in advertisements and music videos.

2. The Bible is full of religious imagery, which is often proclaimed in the Sunday readings. On the way home from Mass, intentionally play with religious imagination. Try something like this: "I wonder what *kind* of fish Jesus multiplied when he fed all those people?" or "Do you think they called the bread Jesus multiplied, *Wonder* Bread?"

3. Evoke stories. They are often the best resources for exercising religious imagination. Any story with certain themes will do; it doesn't have to be a biblical or religious story. Whenever your teen tells a story, don't interrupt until he or she finishes. Then gently ask the kinds of questions that help your teen take the story to a deeper level where spiritual themes can be discussed, such as, "Are you saying that the main character believed that God wanted her to . . .?" or "You mean they were forced to choose between two things—both of which were wrong?" or "So what would you have done if you were in that situation?"

4. Keep this as your motto and you'll find plenty of moments of grace with which you can help your teen exercise his or her religious imagination: *The present is sacred, and the ordinary is holy.* Pay attention to daily events in a way that respects and expects God's presence in the mundane and in the now. By doing so, you will be there to help your teen name "a-ha" moments when he or she is inspired or enlightened by a thought or an experience of mystery. You will also notice when your teen has "Thank you, Jesus," moments when he or she *senses* God's presence and help. And you can be there to help your teen imagine his or her

way through the "I blew it" moments when he or she discovers that a religious truth or belief confronts something he or she has said or done.

5. For many teens contemporary music, movies, and TV shows can often contain spiritually strong messages. It's all because of religious imagination that young people recognize this dimension of the culture. Encourage your teen to share his or her insights with you.

Celebrating

> *O come, let us sing to the LORD;*
>   *let us make a joyful noise to the rock of our salvation!*
> *Let us come into his presence with thanksgiving;*
>   *let us make a joyful noise to him with songs of praise!"*
>
> Psalm 95:1–2

Introducing the Skill

Young adolescents love to party. It's one of the gifts they bring to the rest of us. Unfortunately, they sometimes don't know how to "party healthy," and they don't think adults can help them. God expects us to celebrate the good times. Celebrating with dancing, music, food, and holiday festivals has always been a tradition among people of God. Somewhere along the way, some Catholics haven't developed (or have lost the ability to) celebrate in healthy and joyful ways.

Your teen and his or her peers know how to celebrate; they just need your encouragement to use their imagination in finding healthy ways to celebrate. In building the skill of Celebrating, your role is *to identify ordinary occasions as a reason to celebrate* and *encourage healthy celebrations* as a way of nurturing the spirit.

In the space below, list three ordinary occasions that you can convince your teen are worth celebrating, and suggest a positive way to celebrate each occasion. One example is listed for you.

Occasion	**Way(s) to Celebrate**
Completion of English report	Sharing your teen's favorite dessert

For Yourself

1. Describe a time when you enjoyed a good celebration.

2. What's the key ingredient for you to enjoy a good celebration?

3. Describe a time when you were disappointed by the nature of a celebration.

4. Describe a time when a celebration nurtured your spirituality.

5. For you, what's the difference between *healthy* and *unhealthy* celebrations?

On a scale of 1–10 (10 being the highest), how easily and often do you celebrate the good things in life? Explain.

What good thing should you celebrate ASAP, and how can you do so in a healthy way?

Using the Skill

1. To reinforce in your teen a healthy sense of celebrating, you need to explain how celebrating can nurture his or her spirit.

   - Celebrating is a way of giving thanks and showing gratitude for the many good things one has been given or accomplished.
   - Celebrating can help a person develop an awareness of God's presence in his or her life.
   - The practice of healthy celebrating helps a person develop the virtue of joy, which the Bible calls a fruit of the Spirit.

2. Celebrating can also cause a conflict between you and your teen. We live in a culture that equates celebrating with total freedom—freedom from worries, rules, laws, and morality. Make sure you are a voice that insists on maintaining structure, limits, and moral values when it comes to celebrating. When adolescents struggle with how they can explain their parents' "unreasonable" restrictions, tell them to tell their friends, "That's the way my parents think, and even though

I think it's old-fashioned, I can't change their thinking." Even though they'll never admit it, adolescents appreciate boundaries and guidelines.

Your teen gets a phone call at 7 o'clock Friday night. Then, while still on the phone, excitedly asks you whether he or she can go over to a friend's house for a party. You ask if the parents will be home. Your teen says yes. You ask to speak to the parents, but your teen says that the parents are not available to come to the phone because they are out buying food for the party. You want to know which of your teen's friends will be at the party. "Everyone," replies your teen. When you start asking if specific friends (whose parents you trust) will be there, your teen responds with "I'm not sure," "I dunno," and "I don't think so." You have a very uneasy feeling about the party. You tell your teen that he or she can't go. You are not comfortable making a snap decision at the last minute. Your teen mumbles, grumbles, and complains to the caller with "My mother . . . My father . . . ," hangs up the phone, and storms away into his or her bedroom. Fifteen minutes later your teen joins you and the rest of the family in front of the TV and asks, "Where's my popcorn?" as if nothing ever happened.

What happened here? By insisting on structure and limits and by trusting your instincts, you actually relieved your teen from a stressful and risky situation, and at the same time you allowed your teen to save face in front of his or her friend.

Chapter ③

Moral **Decision** Making

Social Analysis

Forming Conscience

Being Accountable

Examining Conscience

Confronting

Discerning What Is Right

These skills help us think things through, demonstrate character, and live a loving and virtuous life. They strengthen the horizontal dimension of our spirituality— our relationships with others.

Social Analysis

> *May the God of steadfastness and encouragement grant you to live in harmony with one another, in accordance with Christ Jesus.*
>
> Romans 15:5

Introducing the Skill

Because of our call to be socially responsible, we as Christians have a responsibility to practice the skill of Social Analysis. Jesus himself modeled this skill. From the beginning until the end, he called his followers to be aware of cultural values and the condition of those who struggle because of them.

This skill challenges us to look beyond our own lives to issues and situations that are affecting others. Social Analysis is a sequence of four steps: Look, Listen, Ask, and Act.

LOOK

up from what you are doing and see what is going on in the world.

into the issues people are talking about by reading the newspaper or watching or listening the news.

behind the information to see *why* people are involved in an issue.

beyond what is printed or broadcast on TV or radio for other information or opinions.

LISTEN

before you make up your mind.

to what people you trust are saying.

for what the Church and the Bible may have to say.

to what is being said by people you don't know.

ASK

questions to get more information: Why does the situation exist? What contributes to it? Who can influence it?

yourself to spend time thinking about an issue.

God by spending time in prayer.

about the consequences: Who is hurt? Who is helped? What would Jesus do?

ACT

by expressing your opinion.

on a situation when you have an opportunity to do something.

locally by doing something.

in writing so people become aware.

with a group to get more done.

for those involved by praying.

For Yourself

1. Place a check mark by any of these statements that are "very true" about you.

○ I read the newspaper or listen to or watch the news regularly.

○ I ask others for their opinions regarding current events.

○ I am intentionally learning what the Church and the Bible have to say.

○ I know what I believe and what I am willing to stand up for.

○ I make it a habit of asking God for wisdom and guidance in understanding current issues.

○ I look for opinions that are not being widely publicized.

○ I listen to other people's opinions before making up my mind.

○ I look for the reasons behind current events.

○ I pray for those involved in world events and for world leaders.

2. Which aspect of Social Analysis seems to be your strength?

3. Which aspect of Social Analysis do you need to work on the most?

4. Make some notes on specific ways you might Look, Listen, Ask, and Act with each of the following issues:

- The Catholic Church proposes that parishes with more resources partner with those parishes that have less for an exchange of gifts.

- Every kind of freedom of speech will be allowed on the Internet.

- A proposal is in place that will make the ownership of all guns illegal.

- Prayer will be allowed in public schools when led by a teacher.

- The United States will stop protecting other countries.

Using the Skill

1. Of all the Skills for Christian Living, this may actually be the easiest to reinforce by deliberately raising issues for social analysis. Using current events, apply the four steps of Social Analysis.

2. When your teen is your age, would you want him or her to remember you as someone who "always forced me to think"? If so, what practice can you begin to do now to make this happen?

Forming Conscience

Happy are those who find wisdom,
  and those who get understanding,
for her income is better than silver,
  and her revenue better than gold.
She is more precious than jewels,
  and nothing you desire can compare with her.

Proverbs 3:13–15

Introducing the Skill

If your teen were to form his or her conscience about the following topics, where would he or she go for information? What would help him or her make a decision regarding these issues?

1. Underage drinking

2. Buying music with lyrics that glorify violence

3. Exploring an inappropriate Web site

The skill of Forming a Conscience must first be about searching for wisdom. Wisdom acts as a compass, guiding us through the unexpected, the stormy, the troublesome, the dangerous, and the inviting as we navigate through life.

For Catholics there are four basic sources of wisdom:
- the Bible
- the teachings of the Catholic Church
- science, or other sources of physical proven fact
- the community

Sometimes all four sources agree. Sometimes they do not. For example, the fact that an action is legal, does not mean it is morally correct. When faced with a situation in which one or more sources seem to conflict, we can do the following: (1) remember that God wants us to form a good conscience; (2) know that God wants us to trust the wisdom of the Church and Scripture in areas not supported by science or the community; and (3) pray for the guidance of the Holy Spirit.

For Yourself

1. Rate yourself on a scale of 1–10 (with 10 being excellent), when it comes to intentionally forming your conscience based on the four sources of wisdom.

2. Pick one of the following topics and write down what you think each of the four sources of wisdom would say about it: *cloning, physician-assisted suicide, war, the Ku Klux Klan, scientific research using living embryos as a source of tissue.*

   Topic:

   The **teachings of the Church** say:

   The **Bible** says:

   Science says:

   The **community's laws and values** say:

Considering the wisdom from these four sources, what would be the most moral decision?

Now write down a topic about which you are interested in forming your conscience.

With what source(s) of wisdom do you want to become more familiar as you study this issue?

With whom would you like to consult on this issue?

Using the Skill

1. Check the following practices that contribute to your teen's practice of forming a conscience:

○ Reading the newspaper or listening to or watching the news regarding current events and moral issues

○ Reading the Bible on his or her own to become familiar with God's word

○ Talking with adults about current events and moral issues

○ Asking questions about current events and moral issues

○ Seeking out the Church's teachings on moral issues

○ Seeking wisdom by taking time and making an effort to identify moral issues and situations he or she faces

○ Spending time in prayer and solitude when making a decision regarding what is right

Overall, what would you say about your teen regarding the forming of his or her conscience?

2. It might help to occasionally remind your teen that not everyone has the opportunity, or takes advantage of the opportunity, to inform his or her conscience. There is also a difference in a conscience that has been formed as a result of passive indoctrination by society, culture, family, and media versus the conscience one has actively *informed* by intentionally seeking wisdom.

3. Encourage prayer. Your teen, like most adolescents, already has a relationship with God. Sometimes the wisest thing to do is to bring an issue before God and listen to his response.

4. Raise moral issues for discussion as a regular family practice. Raise an issue over dinner, in the car, or during a commercial. Play devil's advocate once in a while just to sharpen your teen's thinking. After the conversation, be sure to let him or her know why you took the position you did.

5. Practice listening skills when your teen is trying to articulate his or her opinions. Don't immediately agree or disagree. Ask questions that summarize what you think your teen said, such as "So you are saying . . . , right?"

6. Initiate discussions on moral issues with your teen and his or her friends. Ask them what they see as moral issues faced by youth and adults. Listen to their thoughts on moral and immoral role models. Comment appropriately.

Being Accountable

> *Owe no one anything, except to love one another; for the one who loves another has fulfilled the law. The commandments . . . are summed up in this word, "Love your neighbor as yourself."*
>
> Romans 13:8–9

Introducing the Skill

What do you honestly think your teen would do in each of the following situations?

1. While at a friend's house after school, your teen is offered a beer.

2. Your teen's younger sibling needs help with homework, but your teen promised a friend that he or she would go to the friend's soccer game.

3. One of your teen's friends confided in your teen that he or she is thinking about running away from home. The friend has asked your teen not to tell anyone.

All young adolescents have a number of people from whom they want approval. Consider these people your teen's personal advisors. Your teen is faced with daily demands and decisions. The skill of Being Accountable centers on the nature of your teen's imagined response from his or her personal advisors. When it comes to right and wrong, your teen will feel a sense of accountability if his or her personal advisors are virtuous people.

To enforce Being Accountable:

1. Help your teen identify a friend or family member for each of the following: a truthful person, a wise person, a loving person, a prayerful person, an unselfish person, a patient person, and others who represent virtues. This will help your teen maintain imaginary advisors who include people of God.

2. Help your teen *imagine* what advice or feedback he or she would receive from virtuous people regarding the decisions and demands your teen faces daily. This will force him or her to consider healthy and moral perspectives.

3. Recall the values Jesus taught. Encourage your teen to be accountable to Jesus.

For Yourself

Take a moment to think about persons who comprise your imaginary advisors by reflecting on the following:

1. Write down the initials of those persons you would choose as your imaginary advisors:

2. Check off any of the following persons who can be found within the group you choose.

   O A truthful person   O An unselfish person

   O A prayerful person   O A wise person

   O A loving person   O A courageous person

3. Think of three important moral decisions you have recently made or will have to make soon. Name the situations, and then describe for yourself the advice or feedback you would get from your imaginary advisors.

A work-related situation:

A family situation:

A relationship with a friend, regarding:

Using the Skill

1. Young adolescents generally don't want to practice being accountable. So don't expect your teen to always be open to your coaching. Expect resistance and reluctance often when you approach this skill with your teen. Don't give up.

2. Your teen knows what Jesus taught. Don't be afraid to remind him or her of those values.

3. Encourage your teen's attempts and failures in being accountable with this rationale: When you practice being accountable, you strengthen your spiritual life and your character.

4. If you want your coaching to have credibility and power, hold yourself accountable. For example:

   Remind the cashier when he or she accidentally charges you less than the correct price. Don't try to "get away with it." If your teen is with you, let him or her know why you did so. "I knew the correct price, and it would have been wrong to pretend I didn't know it."

   Apologize to your teen the next time you say something out of anger. If you and your friends acted inappropriately at a ballgame, party, or some other group event, address the action with your teen. "I (We) didn't handle things well yesterday when I (we) . . ."

   Be prepared to be held accountable by your teen. Rather than react with defensiveness or anger, use it as a teachable moment. Also, be open to mutual accountability with your teen and acknowledge when either your expectations or your teen's expectations have not been met.

5. Take the two-handed approach to reinforcing this skill: with one hand, remind your teen to be accountable; with the other hand, recognize when your teen does practice accountability and give him or her specific praise.

Examining Conscience

Always be ready to make your defense to anyone who demands from you an accounting for the hope that is in you; yet do it with gentleness and reverence. Keep your conscience clear, so that, when you are maligned, those who abuse you for your good conduct in Christ may be put to shame.

1 Peter 3:15–16

Introducing the Skill

Examining Conscience is a skill that helps your teen recognize his or her right and wrong attitudes and actions. It helps him or her identify whom he or she has helped or hurt, the effects of hurtful words and actions, how he or she might repair relationships, and what to do in order to make more virtuous choices in the future.

A student spreads a rumor about another classmate. Your teen hears the person spreading the rumor, knows it's false, but doesn't stick up for the truth. The victim of the rumor finds out and confronts **both** *the person spreading the rumor and your teen. Your teen comes to you, angry at the victim, and says, "I didn't do anything wrong!"*

When you help your teen examine his or her conscience in this situation, remember that there are two kind of sins: sins of commission and errors of omission. The teen spreading the rumor obviously did the wrong thing, but your teen chose not to do the right thing. The first teen's sin was one of commission; your teen's sin was one of omission.

Therefore, this skill is always about asking two honest questions about past actions and current situations: "When did I hurt someone?" and "When did I fail to help someone?" Because young adolescents are still concrete thinkers, remind your teen that we help or hurt others with *words, actions,* and *thoughts.*

An examination of conscience consists of the following action: *Admit* what you *commit* and what you *omit.*

Hearing the benefits of the different skills related to spiritual growth helps young people better understand the skill. So you may want to find a casual way to point out to your teen that the more skilled he or she becomes at examining his or her conscience, the more

- he or she will be a person of character.
- he or she will feel better about himself or herself.
- he or she will be more at peace with God.
- he or she will find it easier to check his or her words, thoughts, and actions before making statements or decisions.

For Yourself

1. Take a moment to practice examining your own conscience by customizing this question for each situation and then reflecting on the events.

   When,   Who,   How (circle one)

   have I

   hurt,   failed to help (circle one)

   someone with my

   words,   thoughts,   actions (circle one)?

2. Examining conscience can serve as the first step toward reconciliation. How might you move toward reconciliation with the situation you listed in the previous question?

3. What do you find to be the hardest thing about examining conscience? (check one)

   ○ Too busy   ○ Fear

   ○ Complicated   ○ Forgetting to focus
     relationships   on omissions

   ○ Pride   ○ Moral apathy

Using the Skill

1. Sometimes examining conscience calls to mind sin—a word we usually use to describe an attitude or action that violates God's law. Adolescents, like all of us, sin. Point out the moral seriousness of hurtful words, thoughts, or actions when appropriate. But don't identify everything as sinful. If you do, the concept of sin will lose its power to evoke serious thought and reflection with your teen.

2. Encourage your teen to set aside time to examine his or her conscience. Perhaps you can encourage this as part of Keeping the Lord's Day or as part of your adolescent's prayer before sleeping.

3. Encourage your teen to find a favorite place for this kind of reflection.

4. Remember that an examination of conscience should lead to reconciliation. The recognition of sin must be followed by active reconciliation. Encourage your teen to apologize to and reconcile with anyone he or she has hurt. Reconciliation can be filled with emotional, social, and religious rewards for your teen and his or her peers.

5. Use the Church Seasons of Advent and Lent to participate in communal celebrations of the Sacrament of Reconciliation.

6. Learn how to stimulate this skill with two casual but provocative questions: "How did you hurt so and so?" and "How did you fail to help so and so?" These two questions can be asked anywhere and anytime, such as while watching TV, running errands, cooking dinner, or sitting in the bleachers. You can ask these two questions while listening to your teen explain or complain about a situation, or you can initiate these questions as you confront your teen about his or her words, thoughts, and actions.

Confronting

> *"If another member of the church sins against you, go and point out the fault when the two of you are alone. If the member listens to you, you have regained that one. But if you are not listened to, take one or two others along with you, so that every word may be confirmed by the evidence of two or three witnesses."*
>
> Matthew 18:15–16

Introducing the Skill

A s you can see from the Gospel passage above, Confronting was a Skill for Christian Living that Jesus himself thought was important enough to address. Confronting requires both kindness and courage. Confronting in this manner does not rob another person of dignity, nor does it water down an issue that needs to be addressed.

When reinforcing the skill of Confronting, focus on three different areas: *verbal, nonverbal,* and *interpersonal.*

Verbal   Be aware of the words and sentences you speak when confronting. Choose your words carefully.

- If possible, make a positive statement about the person before naming the problem behavior.
- Begin by naming the behavior (instead of the person) that is the problem. Say "Cheating is like stealing" instead of "You cheated yesterday."
- Use "I" language whenever possible. Say "I feel hurt when I hear things like that," rather than, "You hurt me when you say things like that."
- Always be specific about the details of the wrongdoing or hurtful action. "Rumors hurt. Kelly was crying over a false rumor about her that was told to Emma."
- Speak clearly and calmly; avoid yelling and arguing.

Nonverbal

Be aware of the way your body gives messages through facial expression, physical position, and posture.

- Approach the other person or group with a calm expression rather than a tense or angry one.

- Sit or stand at eye level with the other(s) instead of standing over someone who is sitting.

- Try to maintain a relaxed physical position. Avoid clenching your fist or crossing your arms.

Interpersonal

Consider the needs and feelings of the person or group you are about to confront.

- Decide what time and place will work best. When possible, talk privately with the person or group—as Jesus suggested. We should not embarrass or shame a person when confronting him or her.

- Keep in mind the wisdom behind the saying "Hate the sin, but love the sinner." This will help you address the wrongdoing while not attacking the person who messed up.

- Remember that the Christian way of confronting involves kindness as well as courage.

For Yourself

1. For each of the following situations, how would you practice the verbal, nonverbal, and interpersonal elements making up the skill of Confronting?

   - *Your good friend, the parent of three school-aged children, has been going to the casino boat to gamble, leaving less and less time for her spouse and kids. "Therapy," she explains.*

- *The parents of your teen's friend are sponsoring a high school graduation party for their senior. They are allowing the kids to drink at the party as long as someone sober agrees to serve as the designated driver. "It's much safer than having them drink at the hotel and then trying to drive home," say the parents.*

- *While standing in line waiting to place his or her order, a friend of yours tells a racist joke in front of your teen and his or her peers. Your friend, while laughing, asks if you get the joke.*

- *A colleague at work continually and deliberately avoids doing his job by making excuses and deceiving management. He now asks if you think he has done anything wrong.*

- *Your teen's coach gets angry during the heat of the games and is verbally abusive to the players.*

Do your proposed actions focus on behaviors or the individual?

Do you see yourself being sensitive to the other person regarding the time and place for confronting? If not, go back to some of these situations and think how you might improve your approach to confronting the situation and person involved.

2. Now take a real-life situation that you want to confront, and make yourself a few notes as to the best way to do it in light of what we have discussed:

Situation:

Verbal:

Nonverbal:

Interpersonal:

Using the Skill

1. It may be helpful to remember the difference between the skill of Being Accountable and the skill of Confronting when reinforcing this with your teen. Being accountable is a form of challenging *yourself* to moral living; confronting is a form of challenging *someone else.*

2. Some adolescents will confront someone only when the pain they suffer over the wrongdoing hurts badly enough. By then, the teen may be full of anger, which can spill over as he or she tries confronting. Therefore, coach your teen into taming his or her anger before confronting. Otherwise the confrontation will only make things worse.

3. Because of the danger of pent-up anger, it's a good idea to encourage your teen to exercise confronting early on. Your teen will say, "It's no big deal. If it gets worse, I'll say something." You might want to suggest that confronting early is better, "before it becomes a really big deal with a lot of anger and frustration behind it."

4. As with all the other tough skills connected to relationships and conflict, be extra alert to catching your teen's everyday attempts at confronting whenever and wherever they occur. Praise the courage behind the attempt and whatever positive verbal, nonverbal, and interpersonal elements you can find. Only then should you offer suggestions on how your teen can improve his or her practice of confronting.

5. Intentionally model this skill when confronting your teen, a rude salesperson, a dishonest coworker, and so on. Ask for feedback from your teen on how well you did. Apologize when you don't do a good job of confronting; this will serve to send a message to your teen regarding the importance you place on this skill.

6. Casually offer hypothetical situations as a way for your teen to practice the skill. If you notice that the local radio station is running a commercial that makes fun of a certain ethnic group, you could spontaneously ask your teen, "Now what's the best

way for me to confront that commercial?" If your neighbors are letting their dog run around in your yard, you might ask aloud, "What's the best way to approach Mr. and Mrs. Gray about their dog?"

Discerning What Is Right

> *"But the Advocate, the Holy Spirit, whom the Father will send in my name,*
> *will teach you everything, and remind you of all that I have said to you."*
>
> John 14:26

Introducing the Skill

Sometimes it's really clear what's right and wrong. Sometimes it is a bit more difficult to tell. The skill of Discerning What Is Right can be very helpful to your teen's moral life.

Are any of these acts wrong no matter what? If so, which one(s)?

Your teen has sexual intercourse.

Your teen cheats on a test.

Your teen takes your credit card and uses it to purchase clothes on the Internet.

Could any of these wrong acts be less wrong depending on the circumstances? If so, give an example.

Here are three things you need to remember when reinforcing this skill:

- the *act*
- the *intention*
- the *circumstances*

The Church teaches that some acts are wrong no matter what, such as fornication, murder, blasphemy, perjury, and adultery. That's what is called *objective morality.* But the Church also teaches that there are other times when the act can be wrong, but the intention of the person committing the act can be a good one. And sometimes the circumstances in which a person commits a wrong act may put the wrong act in a different light.

Your teen and his or her peers often overstate the value of intentions and circumstances in discerning right from wrong. Intentions and circumstances cannot automatically serve as excuses for acts that are wrong.

For Yourself

1. Try discerning right from wrong by imagining yourself in each of these situations:

   - *One of your closest friends confides in you that he or she is falling in love with another person but hasn't told his or her spouse. "I never expected this. I don't want to say anything yet, because maybe it won't last. Do you think I'm doing the right thing?"*

   - *It's tax time. You are thinking about exaggerating how much you've given in cash donations because you figure that you've forgotten to claim other deductions somewhere along the line.*

   - *Your sister is dying and has not yet told your seriously ill mother. Your mother asks about your sister's health. You lie and say, "Doctors haven't figured it out yet."*

- *A group of your coworkers is figuring out a way to stay at the hotel a day longer than necessary at an upcoming out-of-state conference in order to do some sightseeing. They plan on making it look like work so that the company can cover the expenses. They want to know if you think this is okay.*

What can you say about your way of discerning right from wrong?

2. Is there a real-life situation in which you need to discern right from wrong? If so, indicate it in some way here and evaluate the act, intention, and circumstances involved.

Situation:

Act:

Intention(s):

Circumstances:

What's your conclusion?

Using the Skill

1. Whenever you can, find a way to help your teen take the time needed to think through the three different elements in discerning right from wrong. If necessary, establish a motto such as *Just a minute, let me think.* Tape it to the refrigerator.

2. The skill of Discerning What Is Right is also a helpful teaching tool *after your teen discerns poorly.* Often, you can help your teen analyze his or her decision by discussing the specific act, intention, and circumstances.

3. Learn to speak in shorthand with your teen regarding this skill. It will make it easier for your teen to remember. From time to time, when discussing the morality of situations and decisions, say things like, "The intention doesn't outweigh *that* act," or "Circumstances matter."

4. Sometimes adolescents will give up on discerning right from wrong because it can be mentally and emotionally draining. Understand your teen's lack of patience but keep encouraging him or her.

5. When an act is inexcusable, you need to have the moral courage to say so.

6. Think of the dream your heart holds for your teen. Now think of all that can threaten the fulfillment of that dream. The choices adolescents make can be difficult. Part of your legacy can be the fierceness with which you encouraged your teen to discern right from wrong.

Chapter

Emotional
Management

Staying Hopeful

Handling Anger

Lamenting

Expressing Affection

Dealing with Anxiety

Letting Go

*Emotional management skills help us deal
with strong feelings that have a direct impact
on our moral life. These skills strengthen the
internal dimension of our spirituality by helping
us deal with strong feelings.*

Staying Hopeful

> *"Come to me, all you that are weary and are carrying heavy burdens, and I will give you rest. Take my yoke upon you, and learn from me; for I am gentle and humble in heart, and you will find rest for your souls. For my yoke is easy, and my burden is light."*
>
> Matthew 11:28–30

Introducing the Skill

Our faith gives us many reasons to be hopeful. Jesus' death and resurrection gives us the best reason to have hope—in this life and the next. But even if we know the sources of our hope, staying hopeful when bad things happen is an entirely different task. And bad things often happen to adolescents, such as, "He didn't call me like he said he would," "They went to the movies without telling me," "We're moving," "My grandfather has cancer," and "I didn't make the team."

The skill of Staying Hopeful, like almost all emotional management skills, involves the three-step process of Name It, Tame It, Claim It. *Name it* means identifying the feeling or thought. *Tame it* means managing the emotion or gaining control over the emotion by admitting that you are experiencing it. *Claim it* means trying to put the emotion to productive use. Your teen can practice this process when working with any emotion.

Once your adolescent names the emotion, he or she can tame it by asking three questions: Is this a permanent situation? Do I have the power to change it? Is this the way things usually happen to me?

Let's say your teen is falling behind in English class:

Name it: *"I feel like giving up. I'm sure the teacher and the rest of the class think I'm stupid."*

Tame it: Is it permanent? *"Not necessarily."* Do I have the power to change it? *"I don't know. Maybe I could if I ask the teacher for extra help."* Is this typical? *"Not really. I usually do well in school."*

Claim it: *"I get a little behind and then it snowballs.* Or, *"I keep thinking that I can make it up on the next assignment. But the next assignment turns out to be as hard as the first one!"* Or, *"I get discouraged easily."* So, *"Maybe I should ask for help the first time I get behind."*

For Yourself

Rate yourself by circling *RT* (Really True), *T* (True), or *NT* (Not True).

1. Bad things happen to me and those
I care about.   RT   T   NT

2. I tend to give up easily.   RT   T   NT

3. I usually don't make a good impression
on new people I meet.   RT   T   NT

4. I don't like taking on new tasks.   RT   T   NT

5. If I don't perform well on a project at
work, my boss will give up on me.   RT   T   NT

6. If someone doesn't answer me when
I say hello, I tend to think the person
didn't hear me.   RT   T   NT

7. If something is not going well at work,
I tend to think we can fix it.   RT   T   NT

8. I can usually succeed at a new project.   RT   T   NT

9. In general, I'm a hopeful person.   RT   T   NT

10. God helps me when I need it.   RT   T   NT

Scoring: *Pessimism:* On items 1–5 you may have trouble staying hopeful yourself if you answered *VT* to three or more statements or if you answered *NT* to one or none of them. This can also be the case if you answered *NT* to three or more from items 6–10. *Optimism:* Look at your answers to items 6–10. According to the eighth graders who helped develop this self-assessment, you probably find it easy to stay hopeful if you answered *VT* to three or more of these statements or *NT* to one or none of them. This can also be the case if you answered *NT* to three or more of statements 1–5.

Regardless of your score, try the following exercise.

In which situation might you find yourself losing hope?
(check one)

○ An abusive supervisor

○ An unresponsive son
  or daughter

○ A terminally ill parent

○ Insensitive coworkers

○ Lack of time for
  personal interests

○ A consistently
  unmanageable workload

○ An irresponsible brother
  or sister

○ Your teen's learning
  disability

○ An unhealthy relationship

○ Other

You have named those situations in which you are losing hope.
Now tame the feeling by answering these three questions about
the situation:

Is it permanent or temporary?

Do I have the power to change it?

Is this typical of what happens to you?

Claim the feeling by identifying how you can put this experience
to positive use or what you have learned from this experience.

Using the Skill

1. When you sense your adolescent is leaning toward hopelessness, casually lead him or her through the three steps of staying hopeful. The trick is to lead him or her through the steps while both of you are doing something else at the same time, such as while you're in the car or watching TV together. Ask the three questions involved in taming hopelessness: "Is this temporary or permanent?" "Do I have the power to change it?" and "Is this typical?" You can ask the questions in a way that allows your teen to give a yes-or-no answer, while still leaving open the possibility for actual sentences and discussion.

2. Remember that people who struggle most often with feelings related to hopelessness are those who tend to think that many unfortunate situations are permanent, unchangeable, and typical. Help work against such thinking by pointing out the temporary nature of situations or by helping him or her rectify the situation.

3. During times of loss and grief, the process of regaining hope takes time. The best thing to do in these situations is to offer companionship, prayer, and silent togetherness, while still participating in the regular activities of life.

4. Faith matters. Don't use faith lightly, but sometimes it is healthy and helpful to sincerely look your teen in the eyes and encourage him or her to "put this in God's hands, just for a few days." This will give your teen a chance to trust in the mystery of God, draw strength from his or her spirituality, and turn his or her attention away from this situation to focus on something else—again, "just for a few days."

Handling Anger

> *Be angry but do not sin; do not let the sun go down on your anger....*
>
> Ephesians 4:26

Introducing the Skill

Anger is normal, and as the passage above implies, anger is not bad. What we do with our anger, however, is the issue. Everyone gets angry, and we all need help managing our anger. Some people are slow to get angry and quick to forgive. Others get angry quickly and hold grudges for prolonged periods of time. Some hold in their anger and then use drugs or starve themselves to cope with their repressed feelings. Others forget what they were angry about moments after they explode. We need to learn how to manage the extremes of emotion we experience.

Write down a word or a symbol that recalls a time your teen handled his or her anger well.

Do the same for a time in which your teen didn't handle his or her anger very well.

As with Staying Hopeful, there is a three-step process that you can help your teen practice: Name it, Tame it, Claim it. Here's how the process can work when it comes to Handling Anger:

- Name all the emotions you are feeling. You may discover that you are actually feeling embarrassed or rejected instead of angry. Taming rejection or embarrassment is different from taming anger.
- Taming anger involves two parts: *wonder* and *wait*. Encourage your teen to take a moment when he or she is angry and *wonder* whether he or she has all the facts. Wonder if the person or group he or she is angry with actually meant what was said or done. Wonder whether he or she is making too much of the situation.

Then tell your teen to *wait* before he or she says or does anything. Allow time to get through the rush of anger. (There is an African proverb that states, "When anger knocks at your door, wait until tomorrow before you let it in.") Encourage your teen to distract himself or herself by doing something else for a short time. For example, he or she might count to ten or twenty, take a walk, listen to his or her favorite music, pray for God's guidance to help him or her see the big picture. *Wonder* and *wait* are the taming techniques that make the skill of Handling Anger different from managing any other emotion.

• Claiming anger means finding a way to put the emotion to good use. Claiming anger can consist of reminding yourself to be more careful about something the next time, or to reaffirm what is right and what is wrong. If claimed, anger can actually help your teen clarify what is really important and motivate him or her to do what is right.

For Yourself

1. How do you handle anger? (Circle the choice that applies most when you deal with feelings of anger.)

Bury my feelings deep inside   Control the anger
Often lose my temper   Allow the anger to control me
Blame others

2. Recall a time when you didn't handle your anger very well. Looking back, what could you have done to handle it better?

3. Recall a time when you handled your anger really well. What was the key to the way you handled your anger then?

4. How can you improve your skill of handling anger?

5. Think of a recent situation that made you angry. Practice applying the Naming, Taming, and Claiming steps.

Name it: The dominant emotion I feel/felt about this situation is/was

Tame it: I wonder if

I can practice waiting by

Claim it: This situation and my anger show me that

Using the Skill

1. Rate how well your teen handles anger. On a scale of 1–5 (1 being "strongly disagree," 5 being "strongly agree") respond to the following:

_____ My teen doesn't control his or her anger, it controls him or her.

_____ My teen doesn't get angry very easily.

_____ He or she gets angry only at certain people.

_____ He or she gets angry, but handles it well.

_____ My teen keeps his or her anger bottled up inside.

_____ Other people can tell when he or she is angry.

_____ He or she regrets a lot of things said or done in anger.

_____ My teen gets angry easily, but blows it off quickly.

_____ He or she gets angry and keeps grudges.

_____ My teen has hurt me and other family members out of anger.

In the future, what signs would you look for to indicate that your teen is improving his or her ability to handle anger?

2. Share with your teen your personal experiences of handling anger poorly and handling it well.

3. Besides coaching your teen on the skill steps for Handling Anger, remind him or her of the following truths regarding anger:

- The feeling of anger is normal and can be used in a positive way, for example, Jesus displayed anger. (See Matthew 21:12–13, Mark 11:15–16, Luke 19:45–46, and John 2:14–16.)

- Never be afraid to recognize what you are experiencing emotionally.

- You need to handle your anger rather than do something hurtful or destructive with it.

- If you don't handle your anger, you will become a victim of it (by letting it dictate your next action, words, or decision).

Lamenting

And about three o'clock Jesus cried with a loud voice, "Eli, Eli, lema sabachthani?" that is, "My God, my God, why have you forsaken me?"

Matthew 27:46

Introducing the Skill

We read in Scripture that Jesus wept in times of sadness, such as at the tomb of his friend Lazarus. (See *John 11:35*.) We know that he was also sometimes frustrated by the resistance of some of the Pharisees to his message. Lamenting is an honest expression of pain, anger, grief, and frustration. Today life offers us many challenges. Things happen that cause us pain, and sometimes we will make mistakes that will hurt us. Learning to practice the skill of Lamenting can help us be honest with God and honest about our emotions of pain, anger, grief, and frustration.

Which of these statements of teens sound like a lament, and which sound like a complaint? Use *L* and *C* to indicate how these statements sound to you.

_____ This food is awful. They never have what I like to eat.

_____ I feel awful about getting mad at my mom. Getting angry seems to end up making me and other people feel bad.

_____ My parents have too many rules. They don't let me do anything.

_____ I'm sad about my best friend moving so far away. It just won't be the same without him.

_____ It makes me sick inside to see or hear about people shooting each other. Why can't people get along?

Lamenting is a spiritual excercise in which sadness or pain is expressed. The skill of Lamenting as a prayer form involves two parts.

• First, honestly describe your pain, anger, frustration, or grief.

• Second, express your hope and your faith that God is available to hear and help you.

You can practice lamenting

For yourself: See, O LORD, how distressed I am;
>>> my stomach churns,
>> my heart is wrung within me,
>>> because I have been very rebellious.
>> In the street the sword bereaves;
>>> in the house it is like death.

Lamentations 1:20

For others: The tongue of the infant sticks
>>> to the roof of its mouth for thirst;
>> the children beg for food,
>>> but no one gives them anything.

Lamentations 4:4

For victims of famine, war, and hardship:
>> Our skin is black as an oven
>>> from the scorching heat of famine.
>> Women are raped in Zion,
>>> virgins in the towns of Judah.
>> Princes are hung up by their hands;
>>> no respect is shown to the elders.
>> Young men are compelled to grind,
>>> and boys stagger under loads of wood.
>> The old men have left the city gate,
>>> the young men their music.
>> The joy of our hearts has ceased;
>>> our dancing has been turned to mourning.

Lamentations 5:10–15

Over someone else's wrongdoing: "Jerusalem, Jerusalem, the city that kills the prophets and stones those who are sent to it! How often have I desired to gather your children together as a hen gathers her brood under her wings, and you were not willing!"

Matthew 23:37

Out of anger: O daughter Babylon, you devastator!
Happy shall they be who pay you back
what you have done to us!

Psalm 137:8

Young people often mistakenly assume that, when it comes to things of God, they should grin and bear it. By encouraging your adolescent to practice Lamenting, you free him or her to be real with God about the pain and troubles of life.

For Yourself

1. Take a moment to check out your personal views and practice of Lamenting by placing a T (True) or F (False) before each of the following statements.

   _____ I complain instead of lament.

   _____ I lament a lot.

   _____ I have been reluctant to lament.

   _____ I usually lament for the plight of others.

   _____ I need to lament more.

   _____ I used to think lamenting was like whining.

   _____ I have a special place to go where I can feel at ease lamenting.

   _____ I find lamenting to be a helpful spiritual practice.

   _____ I want to practice lamenting more than I have in the past.

2. Choose one of the following situations and compose a prayer of lamenting. Remember to include both of the skill steps— describe your feelings, and express your hope.

   • Domestic violence—for example, a person abused by a parent or spouse

   • Local injustice—for example, a case of vandalism or a school shooting

- Social injustice—for example, people not allowed to participate fully in society because of their race or gender
- Global injustice—for example, a war that creates innocent victims

3. Now take a situation in your personal life and compose a prayer of lamenting.

Using the Skill

1. Encourage lamenting, not complaining. Be prepared to explain the difference to your teen.

2. Use the newspaper or the TV news as a springboard for lamenting.

3. Occasionally offer a prayer of lamentation as a part of your blessing at meals. Be sure to include an expression of your pain, frustration, anger, or grief as well as your faith and hope in God's understanding.

4. Use the painful experiences that your teen shares with you as situations for which you pray prayers of lament.

5. Stress that lamenting—with the two steps described—is perfectly acceptable to God.

Expressing Affection

Greet one another with a holy kiss.

1 Corinthians 16:20

Introducing the Skill

Expressing affection in appropriate ways has always been an issue. Even Paul felt the need to coach his friends among the first Christians on this issue. No one is more emotional than an adolescent. Hormones, puberty, sexuality, and a longing for friendship make this a skill necessary to master. Ironically, though, there are no set steps for this skill. The situations calling for the appropriate expression of affection are too diverse and dependent upon the quality of the friendships, the culture, and the settings involved. However, we can help set a foundation for our children.

Today there is disagreement and confusion about what constitutes appropriate loving touch. Appropriate behavior shows respect for both the giver and receiver. Discuss with your teen the following appropriate ways to express affection through our words and actions:

Hold hands.
Say "I love you."
Give hugs and affectionate (not passionate) kisses.
Send a friendship card or flowers.
Say "I'm so glad you are my . . ."
Tell others why you admire them (for themselves
    and not just for their achievements).
Put aside everything else and talk.
Write a note, and put it in a lunch bag.
Share a skill or hobby.
Do chores without being asked.
Take time to listen.
Say "I'm sorry" for wrongs.
Give gifts from the heart.
Share your thoughts and feelings.
Cheer up someone who is sad.

Rate each of the following expressions of affection on a scale of 1–5 (1 being "very inappropriate," 5 being "very appropriate").

_____ A boy really likes being around with a girl in his class. So he sneaks up behind her and knocks the books out of her hands.

_____ Two boys are best friends. They are constantly punching and pushing on each other. When a substitute teacher sends them to the office for fighting, the boys both say, "We were just goofing around."

_____ A couple attends a school dance. They kiss during every slow dance.

_____ A girl is sick and out of school for two weeks. A boy in her class sends her a get-well greeting card.

_____ Two girls seem to care about nothing but some boys in their classes. They call the boys on the phone every night.

_____ A girl wants to know a boy in her class better. She asks him if they could sit together at lunch.

Based on your reactions and thoughts about the previous situations and the ones you've seen with your teen, make a list that you could share with your teen on the following.

Things to Keep in Mind When Expressing Affection
1.
2.
3.
4.
5.

For Yourself

1. Use initials, a word, or a symbol to recall a time when you did well expressing affection.

2. Use initials, a word, or a symbol to recall a time when you were not satisfied with the way you expressed affection.

3. Use initials, a word, or a symbol for each of these: Which person or group do you want to express affection to? How will you do so? What do you want to keep in mind this time?

4. Rate your current skill of Expressing Affection on a scale of 1–5 in these areas (1 being "very poor," 5 being "very good").

_____ Expressing affection to your spouse

_____ Expressing affection to other adults in your family

_____ Expressing affection to friends of the same gender

_____ Expressing affection to your child(ren)

_____ Expressing affection to friends of the other gender

_____ Expressing affection to coworkers

_____ Expressing affection to parents or elders

5. In what one area of Expressing Affection do you want to improve?

Using the Skill

1. Here are key points to remember when coaching your teen on Expressing Affection:

   - We all have the need to express affection and to have others express affection to us.

   - There are appropriate and inappropriate ways to express affection.

   - Expressing affection must always start with the belief that every human is sacred and deserves the respect due a child of God.

   - Expressing affection well always includes respect, sensitivity, boundaries, and chastity appropriate to the situation.

   - Expressing affection also includes protecting and defending those in need.

2. Return to the situations at the beginning of this skill and think of the advice you would give your adolescent.

3. Go back to your list of the things to keep in mind when expressing affection. Is there anything else you want to add?

Dealing with Anxiety

"Therefore I tell you, do not worry about your life, what you will eat or what you will drink, or about your body, what you will wear. Is not life more than food, and the body more than clothing? Look at the birds of the air; they neither sow nor reap nor gather into barns, and yet your heavenly Father feeds them. Are you not of more value than they? And can any of you by worrying add a single hour to your span of life?"

Matthew 6:25–27

Introducing the Skill

Children fret; young adolescents *worry*. They worry about getting a good job, losing a parent through death or divorce, getting good grades, relocating, violence, making the team, being included, the environment, and AIDS.

As with most of the other skills related to emotional management, Dealing with Anxiety involves the same three basic steps of Name it, Tame it, and Claim it.

When naming it, be aware that anxiety usually comes from one of four fears: fear of failure, fear of lack of safety, fear of loss or separation, or fear of rejection. It is important to help your teen identify the dominant fear behind his or her anxiety.

When taming it, refer to four *T*s: *Talk* with someone about what you are thinking and feeling. Apply the *talents* God has given you to address the problem. *Trust* God to help you get through it. It is important to remember that God may not spare you from the situation, but he will help you through it. Finally, walk *toward* the anxiety by taking an action, making a decision, developing a plan, and so on. Don't run from the situation, don't deny the situation, and don't obsess over the situation.

Claiming it means finding a positive use for the emotion. What can be learned from this situation of anxiety? How can this experience of anxiety help in being more empathetic to others? Remember that an important aspect of dealing with anxiety is to rely on your relationship with Jesus.

Which of the four Ts in Dealing with Anxiety do you think is most important for your teen? (circle one) Talk   Talents   Trust   Toward

For Yourself

Self-assess your own practice of Dealing with Anxiety. Circle one response per statement.

1. Most of my anxiety comes from my fear of:

   failure   rejection   lack of safety   loss or separation

2. I tame my anxiety most of the time by:

   talking about it   trusting God

   applying my talents to it   walking toward it

3. In general, I don't experience much anxiety.   True   False

4. I usually pray that God will spare me from something instead of giving me the strength to get through it.   True   False

5. When it comes to Dealing with Anxiety, I'd give myself a grade of: A   B   C   D   F

Take a moment to sketch out how you might practice Dealing with Anxiety over something that burdens you.

Name it: Where's it coming from? A fear of:

   failure   rejection   lack of safety   loss or separation

Tame it: To whom can you talk?

Which of your talents can you apply to the situation?

Where and when can you spend time in prayer, trusting God?

What can you do to actively walk toward the situation to control it?

Claim it: What does your anxiety tell you about yourself? What can you learn from this?

Finally, reread the Scripture passage at the beginning of this skill. What do you hear in this statement from Jesus? What feeling can you identify when you read this? What thoughts or conclusions come to your mind from this reading?

Using the Skill

1. Review any anxiety you have noticed in your teen over the last year or so. List here the five most serious or recurrent situations that have caused your teen a lot of anxiety.

   -
   -
   -
   -
   -

   Which fear do you think is the most common source of your teen's anxiety?

Which of the four taming techniques does he or she practice most often—talk with someone, apply his or her talents, trust God, or walk toward the anxiety?

Which of the four taming techniques do you think your teen should practice more often in order to improve his or her skill in Dealing with Anxiety?

Do you think your teen prays for God to spare him or her from situations, or does he or she pray for God's help to get through it? Why do you think this?

2. Besides the four *T*s, reinforce these points in dealing with anxiety:

   - Dealing with anxiety is a spiritual matter. This is one reason the Lord's Prayer at Mass is followed by a prayer asking for God's help with our anxieties.

   - Most people can develop the skill of Dealing with Anxiety.

   - People have been struggling with anxiety throughout history. Jesus made it a point to address this in his teachings (Matthew 6:25–34 and Luke 12:22–31).

   - Walking toward your anxiety means taking action instead of running from or denying your anxiety. Perhaps you can work with your teen to think of ways to help move toward the anxiety. Walking toward the situation means asserting yourself instead of passively hoping the anxiety goes away. Work with your adolescent to think of steps he or she can take to overcome the anxiety.

Letting Go

For I am convinced that neither death, nor life, nor angels, nor rulers, nor things present, nor things to come, nor powers, nor height, nor depth, nor anything else in all creation, will be able to separate us from the love of God in Christ Jesus our Lord.

Romans 8:38–39

Introducing the Skill

Young people know pain. Bad stuff happens all the time while navigating the turbulent waters of adolescence: they lose a friend, make a stupid mistake and pay serious consequences, get ignored when they need and deserve recognition, have something embarrassing happen to them, discover that a friend has lied to them, believe a teacher has been unfair, lose a ball game, get falsely accused, and so on.

While the skill of Dealing with Anxiety centers on *an upcoming or ongoing situation or conflict,* the skill of Letting Go deals with managing emotions over something which has *already happened.* Letting Go consists of overcoming your preoccupation with the situation and replacing it with something new.

When has your teen really struggled with letting go?

What do you remember most about this time?

Letting Go is an important and difficult skill in emotional management. As with most of the other skills in this skill set, it involves the Name it, Tame it, and Claim it process.

Naming it helps you identify exactly what emotion(s) you are feeling—mad, sad, angry, embarrassed, happy, and so on. This step alone can be freeing for anyone unable to let go.

Taming it centers around this spiritual truth of the Paschal mystery: Dying is followed by rising. Every good-bye is followed by a new hello. Therefore, we have to say good-bye to whatever it is we are holding on to and release it to God. Understand that this is a matter of faith. It requires a degree of acceptance, no matter how unfair, painful, or tragic the situation is.

Then you have to say hello to something new. This means being open to replacing what you have released or said good-bye to. If you don't have the energy to or interest in replacing what you have said good-bye to, then you must simply stay open to the next phase. The release-and-replace process of "Say good-bye, say hello" takes time. If you say good-bye too quickly, you will just want to bring it back again. Saying hello too quickly by jumping into a new friendship, hobby, or group can offer a new set of difficulties.

Claiming it in the case of Letting Go almost always involves reaching some conclusions about what your heart holds dear and what you value most in life and in others. It is a dual opportunity to learn from an experience and to better understand the pain of others.

For Yourself

Reflect on your practice of Letting Go by rating yourself on a scale of 1–5 for each of the following statements (1 being "strongly disagree," 5 being "strongly agree").

_____ I don't usually dwell on things that go wrong.

_____ I am able to forgive those who have harmed me.

_____ I have someone with whom I can share my disappointment.

_____ My faith is a source of strength for me in the process of letting go.

_____ I take too long to say good-bye to the feelings of which I should let go.

_____ I say hello too quickly after a good-bye.

_____ Letting go is a spiritual exercise.

_____ The release-and-receive process of Letting Go is hard for me.

_____ I need to improve my skill in Letting Go.

Based on how you have rated yourself above, what aspect of Letting Go do you want to improve on?

Sketch a symbol, word, or initial of something you need to let go.

What is the dominant emotion you feel in letting go of this?

What is the challenge in saying good-bye to this?

What do you need in order to say hello?

When and how can you make this part of your prayer time?

Using the Skill

1. You can help your teen articulate the harmful effects of *not* letting go. The following exercise is a chance to identify some of these effects:

Erica was cut from the basketball team. All of her best friends made the team. She is sure that politics were involved in her being cut. She tells other classmates that two girls made the team only because their parents are good friends with the coach.

Chris thinks about Michelle all the time. He writes her notes in class and calls her every night. He scribbles her name on his notebooks and watches everything she does, even though three weeks ago Michelle told Chris that she just wants to be his friend and nothing more than that.

Six months ago Tim moved to another state. He has not tried to make new friends. Instead he e-mails his old friends. He says that he is bored and unhappy. He is mad at his parents for moving.

What are the effects of not letting go:

for Erica:

for Chris:

for Tim:

What do you think is the hardest thing about Letting Go for your adolescent?

2. Remind your teen that there are certain things to remember about Letting Go.

- The pain of letting go can give some insight into what his or her heart really holds dear.

- Saying good-bye or saying hello too quickly isn't always a good thing. It's okay to take some time with Letting Go.

- Letting Go is a difficult skill to master.

- Letting Go is a spiritual exercise because it involves inner healing and calls you to have faith that God will bring you a new *hello* in his own time.

Chapter 5

Gospel Living

Practicing Empathy

Reconciling

Giving Thanks

Offering Solidarity

Honoring the Body

Resolving Conflict

These skills introduce some of the basic behaviors and practices that are at the core of living the gospel as Jesus taught. They affect all three dimensions of our spirituality— vertical, horizontal, and internal.

Practicing Empathy

[I]f anyone has caused pain . . . you should forgive and console him, so that he may not be overwhelmed by excessive sorrow. . . . I urge you to reaffirm your love for him.

2 Corinthians 2:5, 7–8

Introducing the Skill

Psychologists tell us that empathy is at the heart of our ability to lead moral lives. Empathy is being aware of and sensitive to the thoughts, feelings, needs, and experiences of others. It is the seed of caring. To the degree with which we are able to practice empathy, we can see outside ourselves and listen to the people around us.

Your adolescent is empathetic. Don't be fooled by his or her preoccupation with self or the chaotic way he or she hesitates when making a decision. A tender and sensitive heart lies beneath the exaggerated concerns about appearance, phone calls, and being included. Encourage your teen to practice empathy.

There are two parts to the Christian approach to practicing empathy. Call it *R and R: recognize* how someone is feeling and try to understand his or her reactions, and *respond* in caring and helpful ways. Both aspects are necessary. Recognizing how another feels without responding doesn't help anyone, and responding to another without recognizing how that person feels is robotic.

How would you coach your teen regarding empathy using R and R in the following situations?

1. He or she found out that the parents of a friend are getting divorced.

2. His or her friend scored the winning goal at a soccer game.

3. Your older son's girlfriend just broke up with him.

4. One of your teen's friends is being bullied.

For Yourself

Rate your own ability to practice empathy on a scale of 1–5
(1 being "almost never" and 5 being "almost always").

_____ I use both steps of R and R in my practice of empathy.

_____ I find it difficult to know how to respond to others in need.

_____ I can accurately sense what a person is feeling in
most situations.

_____ I readily practice empathy with friends.

_____ I readily practice empathy with coworkers.

_____ I readily practice empathy with my children.

_____ I readily practice empathy with my spouse.

_____ I readily practice empathy with strangers.

_____ I readily practice empathy with older family members.

_____ I readily practice empathy with my child(ren)'s friends.

Which person(s) in your life comes to mind as a model of
one who shows empathy by practicing R and R?

Describe a time when you were truly blessed by someone
practicing empathy.

What is one thing you want to improve in your own
practice of empathy?

Using the Skill

1. When your family learns about someone's struggle within the community, reinforce the practice of empathy by asking questions like "How do you think she feels?" and "What might we do to help out?"

2. Besides R and R, stress some key points when it comes to practicing empathy:

   • We will enter the kingdom of God by practicing empathy as Jesus taught. (See *Matthew 25.*)

   • Practicing empathy is at the heart of living a love-filled life.

3. Your ability to model the practice of empathy with strangers, friends, and your own family members can set a good example for your teen.

4. As tough as it gets, have the moral courage to point out times when you or your teen failed to practice empathy well.

5. Sometimes the best examples of empathy are done in silence: silent companionship and silently listening to the one in need.

6. Responding with empathy means that we are concerned for the other person more than we are for ourselves.

Reconciling

"So when you are offering your gift at the altar, if you remember that your brother or sister has something against you, leave your gift there before the altar and go; first be reconciled to your brother or sister, and then come and offer your gift."

Matthew 5:23–24

Introducing the Skill

Are either of the following situations good examples of reconciliation? Why or why not?

Your teen hurts your feelings and wants to reconcile. He or she apologizes to you but then says, "I wouldn't be mad at you if you let me do what I want more often."

Your teen and his or her friend have an argument. Your teen knows that the friend feels bad and wants to apologize, but your teen is still upset. When the friend approaches, your teen says, "I'm really mad at you, and I'll forgive you if you do whatever I want for a week."

Jesus' instructions from the Scripture passage indicate that the first Christians had to reconcile with each other in order to continue on the path of spiritual growth. So do we—sometimes even when we are not at fault. Getting a second chance is a gift everyone longs for. You can coach your teen through a four-step process of reconciling that he or she will find easy to remember.

The inscription above Jesus' head on the cross read INRI, meaning "Jesus of Nazareth, King of the Jews." His death reminds us that we have a God who always forgives us and who reminds us that nothing is hopeless. The letters on Jesus' cross can remind your teen of the need for—and the steps involved in—reconciling.

Identify the wrong that was done and the trust that was broken.

No excuses should be made for what happened.

Responsible action is called for.

Identify a goal for strengthening the relationship.

For Yourself

1. Here's a chance to sharpen your own reconciling skills. Pick one or two of the following scenarios and sketch out how you would use the steps for reconciling.

   - You lied to your spouse about not using the credit card, when, in fact, you used it to buy merchandise related to a favorite hobby that your spouse feels you spend too much time and money on.

   - Someone at work circulated a joke that made fun of a coworker's ethnic group and you laughed along.

   - Your father-in-law has a stroke while at your house over the holidays. Your spouse's brothers and sisters call you from out of state for a report from the emergency room. You are stressed by the urgency of the situation and respond with short, to-the-point answers. The family members let your spouse know that they are extremely upset with you for being insensitive and for what they perceived as "withholding information."

   - You came home from work totally exhausted and yelled at your teen for no apparent reason.

2. Now pick a current situation in which you need to practice the skill of Reconciling. Describe the situation, and then write how you can use the INRI skill steps to resolve the situation. Use initials or symbols if you wish.

Situation needing reconciliation:

Identify the wrong act you have been involved in and the trust that was broken.

No excuses. Don't try to explain your part in what happened.

Responsible action. What will you do to make amends?

Identify the goal. Specify what's important to you in this relationship.

Using the Skill

1. Sometimes an adolescent may resist any attempt at reconciliation. In these cases, factors influencing your teen's resistance are not really related to the situation at hand. For clues to the motive for refusing reconciliation, look to such things as past events that may have left an emotional scar, look at how reconciling may appear to the larger peer group, look at previous patterns of wrongdoing, previous rejection, and so on.

2. It may be helpful for you to assess basic tendencies of your teen related to the skill of Reconciling. On a scale of 1–5 (1 being "not true," 5 being "very true"), rate the degree to which each statement is true for your teen.

_____ People who know my teen would say that he or she is quick to forgive.

_____ Even if my teen doesn't cause the problem, he or she usually tries to make up with the other person.

_____ My teen seems to find it easy to ask for forgiveness when he or she is at fault.

_____ My teen doesn't sulk about something for a long time before reconciling.

_____ My teen tries not to make excuses when he or she has done something wrong.

_____ My teen has had several good experiences of reconciling in the past.

_____ My teen is quick to engage in responsible actions that make direct amends for a wrong act.

_____ My teen makes the effort to maintain honest and supportive relationships.

Based on this exercise, what specific aspects of reconciling do you want to work on with your teen?

3. Reflect on parent-teen interactions. How do you and your adolescent react to situations of reconciliation with each other? What makes it difficult to reconcile? What helps you reconcile?

Giving Thanks

> *Rejoice always, pray without ceasing, give thanks in all circumstances; for this is the will of God in Christ Jesus for you.*
>
> 1 Thessalonians 5:16–18

Introducing the Skill

How could each of these young people have done a better job of giving thanks?

A neighbor was kind enough to carpool your teen to the school field trip because your work schedule didn't allow you to go. Your neighbor has done this several times. Upon returning home, your teen gets out of your neighbor's car and heads for the house. You say, "Can you thank Mrs. Brown?" Your teenager continues to the house without breaking stride, opens the front door, and with his or her back to the Brown's car nonchalantly says "Thanks" just before the door closes behind him or her.

Your teen's game has just ended. As is the tradition, one of the parents has a cooler full of drinks waiting for the team as they come to the sidelines. The first player to the cooler asks, "These ours?" The parent nods. The players each reach for a drink and walk away.

The skill of Giving Thanks nurtures our spiritual lives because it makes us take the time to recognize kindness, express our gratitude, or count our blessings. Giving thanks forces us to make a note of the good things in life—both small and large—reminding us of everything that contributes to our happiness.

Here's one way to practice Giving Thanks. Remember the letter *S*.

Stop—Stopping is a respectful way of honoring the situation for which we want to give thanks.

Smile—Smiling is a concrete way of displaying our appreciation.

Say something—Saying something enables us to make personal contact with the other person. You can also say something through a gesture or a gift instead of words.

Store it—Storing it in your memory helps when you forget how kind someone can be, the good times in life, or the blessings of God. By storing it, you can pull out a good memory when you need one.

For Yourself

1. Evaluate your own practice of giving thanks by rating yourself on a scale of 1–5 (1 being low, 5 being high).

   _____ Giving thanks is something I do often.

   _____ I usually stop whatever I'm doing when I want to thank someone.

   _____ I make sure to look the other person in the eye and smile when I give thanks.

   _____ This is the rating my kid(s) would give me for the frequency and manner in which I practice Giving Thanks.

   _____ I make it a point to deliberately express my gratitude with words or a gesture when giving thanks.

   _____ I find myself easily remembering events, moments, or relationships for which I give thanks.

   _____ Giving Thanks is a big part of my conversation with God.

2. When do you find yourself giving thanks to other people?

3. When do you find yourself giving thanks to God?

4. Imagine this situation: Late at night after everyone else is asleep, you come across two old pictures of your cute, happy kids in Halloween costumes. How could you practice the *S* approach to Giving Thanks?

Using the Skill

1. You may want to go back to the two earlier situations and see how the young people could have applied different components of the *S* approach to Giving Thanks. Here are a few new situations to help you work with your teen at the skill of Giving Thanks.

You come home from a tense day at the hospital after your mother's operation. Your teen is on the couch watching TV. As you put down your keys and take off your jacket, you announce with exhaustion and relief, "Grandma's tumor wasn't cancerous. Thank God. It's an answer to my prayers. We're so lucky, you know?" Your teen, aiming the remote at the TV and flicking through channels, says, "Neat," and keeps on flicking.

Three infants are baptized during Mass. The beauty and innocence of these infants touch you. You reach for your teen's hand and whisper that you still remember all the fuss your family made over his or her Baptism. Everybody showed up. You explain that his or her godparents threw a big party, treated everyone to lunch, and continue to send Christmas gifts to this day. Your teen continues looking at the babies being baptized and nods, then turns to you and asks, "Can we stop and get donuts after church?"

Your teen misses three days of school because of the flu, thereby falling further behind in English, in which he or she already has a low grade. You ask your teen to see if the teacher will give him or her some make-up work. The teacher offers to meet with your teen after school for the next three Tuesdays. Your teen explains that there is a conflict with Tuesday afternoons, so the teacher offers to meet on Friday mornings before school. Your teen makes the three Friday morning sessions and pulls the grade up to a B.

2. It's important to remember two things when helping your teen improve at the skill of Giving Thanks.

- Give specific praise to your teen every time he or she does a good job of Giving Thanks. (For example, "It was nice to see you stop and say something when you thanked Mrs. Burke," or "Do you know how good you look when you smile at someone? Your whole face lights up. It says a lot to people when you smile.")

- Model the skill of Giving Thanks as often as possible, so that your teen will notice you doing it.

3. With your teen, adopt a pattern of Giving Thanks in one of a variety of ways, such as:

- Naming something for which they are thankful during the meal blessing.

- Creating a gratitude board on which family members post notes of thanks using sticky notes or using marker on a white eraser board.

Offering Solidarity

> "'[F]or I was hungry and you gave me food, I was thirsty and you gave me something to drink, I was a stranger and you welcomed me, I was naked and you gave me clothing, I was sick and you took care of me, I was in prison and you visited me.'"
>
> Matthew 25:35–36

Introducing the Skill

The skill of Offering Solidarity is all about sharpening your teen's willingness to serve others by *offering* support instead of automatically assuming someone needs or wants support. Sometimes, in the name of service, we can impose ourselves on others and rob them of their own opportunity and dignity. By offering solidarity, we make ourselves available and express our willingness to serve while respecting those in need when they accept or decline.

The Church has always pointed to the Spiritual Works of Mercy—instructing, advising, counseling, and comforting—as concrete actions we can take to offer solidarity.

Take a moment to describe how your teen acts when he or she faces others in need. Circle any of the following that apply.

Tries to understand	Offers comfort
Listens	Expresses availability
Changes the subject	Tries to be kind
Jokes about it	Talks about his or her problems
Doesn't seem to care	Asks what's wrong
Is sympathetic	Becomes uncomfortable

The skill of Offering Solidarity consists of four things—*Eyes, Ears, Hands,* and *Heart.*

1. We must have eyes to see, which means *looking around* and *noticing* who needs help or is being treated unfairly.
2. We must have ears to hear, taking the time to *listen* to those who need help or fair treatment. Listening is the first step toward understanding a problem.
3. We must have hands to help, actually *doing something* to support those in need.
4. We must have hearts to hold, *praying* or *sacrificing* for those in need.

For Yourself

1. Take a moment to rate your own tendencies toward Offering Solidarity by writing *NT* (Not True), *S* (Somewhat True), *T* (True), or *VT* (Very True) before each statement below.

   _____ I'm a good listener.

   _____ I notice the needs of others.

   _____ I make it a priority to help others.

   _____ I'm very understanding.

   _____ I'm a compassionate person.

   _____ I get nervous when it comes to helping others.

   _____ I pray and fast for those who suffer on a regular basis.

   I offered to serve someone within the last two months.
   YES   NO

   Based on your self-assessment, what note do you want to make about your tendencies toward offering solidarity?

2. Help sharpen your own skill at Offering Solidarity by filling in the following boxes.

Have eyes to see: Write down the name of a person or group you know to be in need of support.

Have ears to hear: To whose story do you need to listen, or about what issue do you need to get more information?

Have hands to help: What can you offer to do for a person or group needing support?

Have a heart to hold: In what manner will you pray or fast for the person or group you have listed?

Using the Skill

1. When reinforcing the skill of Offering Solidarity with your teen, think of life as the textbook, full of opportunities to teach and practice this skill.

2. Prayer and fasting are ways the whole family can offer solidarity together for some person or group. If you choose to do this, mark it as a special family moment or activity. For example, "Remember everybody, we'll try to give up eating sweets this Friday for so and so."

3. Your teen needs you to offer solidarity to him or her from time to time. Sometimes offering solidarity with your teen consists of actively helping him or her, but other times it involves being with him or her as a faithful companion, friend, and reliable adult.

4. Pay particular attention to certain areas of your teen's life that may call for solidarity, especially school, sports, physical appearance, goals, and social skills. Help your teen notice such situations.

5. As an activity with your teen or as a family, provide help to someone in need.

6. Find out the organizations and agencies in your area that provide service and discover ways you and your teen might help.

Honoring the Body

[D]o you not know that your body is a temple of the Holy Spirit within you, which you have from God, and that you are not your own?

1 Corinthians 6:19

Introducing the Skill

On a scale of 1–5 (1 being low, 5 being high), rate how much importance your teen places on each of the following activities.

_____ Getting enough sleep

_____ Eating nutritious foods

_____ Praying

_____ Shopping

_____ Doing homework

_____ Exercising

_____ Reading

_____ Spending time together as a family

_____ Watching television

_____ Playing video games

_____ Playing sports

_____ Spending time with friends

_____ Surfing the Internet

_____ Helping out with jobs around the house

_____ Looking good

_____ Having clean clothes

Chances are good that your teen is very concerned about his or her body *and* understands the need to take care of it. But probably your teen does not know how to practice Honoring the Body.

Honoring the Body means showing respect for your body and the bodies of others. It also includes being satisfied with the body you have!

Use the word *respect* to help you reinforce the skill of Honoring the Body.

Rest your body so that you won't get run down.

Exercise regularly to keep your body healthy.

Sexuality is sacred and each person's body should be treated as holy.

Practice good hygiene and stay safe.

Eat properly for health and energy.

Clothe yourself modestly.

Talk about the body with respect, and don't make fun of or use vulgar language when talking about anyone else's.

For Yourself

1. Give yourself a grade from *A*+ to *F* on each of the following practices related to Honoring the Body:

Rest

Exercise

Sexual morality

Practicing good hygiene

Eating healthy

Clothing yourself appropriately

Talking about the body

2. How is Honoring the Body a spiritual activity?

3. What do you wish you could accept about your body?

4. Based on your responses to the previous questions, set one or two goals for yourself to honor your body.

Using the Skill

1. We live in a culture that often dishonors the body by objectifying it and exploiting sexuality. Point out this practice to your teen when you see it on TV, hear it in music, and so on. Your observations and editorial comments will increase your adolescent's ability to notice this practice.

2. Go back to the behaviors associated with *RESPECT,* and target one or two that you want to stress most with your teen.

3. Some adolescents may adopt habits that work against the skill of Honoring the Body—smoking, steroid use, sleep deprivation, drug use, alcohol use. Add three or four more.

4. Make "giving thanks for our bodies" a standard part of your family prayer at meals.

5. To help your teen practice the skill of Honoring the Body, you will sometimes need to spend money and time. Take a minute to think of some reasonable expenses associated with the seven behaviors of *RESPECT.*

Resolving Conflict

"Forgive, and you will be forgiven; give, and it will be given to you. A good measure, pressed down, shaken together, running over, will be put into your lap; for the measure you give will be the measure you get back."

Luke 6:37–38

Introducing the Skill

People get frustrated, tired, angry, and sad during situations of conflict. Two important things to remember about resolving conflicts are that violence within a conflict is never acceptable and that there are some conflicts you cannot and should not try to resolve.

The skill of Resolving Conflict involves healing. By listening to other people's thoughts, opinions, and feelings, we take part in the healing process of peacemaking. But to be successful, one has to navigate the turbulent waters of emotions.

Joshua says he's angry about an incident that happened at school yesterday. As Joshua tells it, "Alex grabbed my new jacket and took off with it. I saw the bus coming to pick us up, and I knew I needed to get on it, but I knew you would be really mad if I came home without my jacket. I ran after Alex to get my jacket back. I yelled at him, but he ran behind the building. The bus monitor saw us running, stopped me, and wrote down our names. So we both have to stay after school tomorrow. Great! That's just what I need. I'm supposed to be at soccer practice then. And I still don't have my jacket back. It's all Alex's fault. If he hadn't called me names, I wouldn't have torn up his math paper and none of this would've happened. But I'll get him back. Just wait."

If Joshua were your child, how would you advise him to resolve the conflict?

Introduce the skill of Resolving Conflict to your teen by stressing these steps:

1. **Listen fully and repeat back.** "So, Joshua, what you are saying is that (repeat it back)," or "I see. You think that . . . (repeat back)." Make sure you listen *carefully* and repeat back *accurately.* Don't try to come up with a solution. Just listen first.

2. **Reduce** the conflict from one large issue to smaller ones, and from multiple issues to just the most important ones. "So what's the best thing to do now: get your jacket back or talk to the bus monitor?" This makes the conflict and its resolution more manageable.

3. **"Peace" it together** with the other person or group by compromising when possible and asserting yourself when you must. "Let's go see Alex and let him know all that's happened. Maybe the two of you can talk to someone together and get this worked out."

4. **Move on.** If you can't seem to resolve the conflict and you've done your best, don't keep thinking about it. Admit that it isn't going to work out and move on. If Alex and Joshua don't work things out, don't force it and don't make it your mission to resolve it.

For Yourself

1. Recall a time when you resolved a conflict well. What was the key to your success?

2. Recall a time when you didn't do a good job resolving conflict. What could you have done differently?

3. Based on the situations presented, which skill steps seem most crucial?

4. Now think of a current situation at work, home, or with friends that needs skillful conflict resolution. Review the skill steps from the previous page, and make some notes regarding how you might carry them out in this case.

Using the Skill

1. In addition to reinforcing the skill steps of Resolving Conflict with your teen, it is wise to remind him or her of some basic truths about how to resolve conflicts.

- Jesus taught us to resolve conflicts.
- Conflict is normal.
- You will get frustrated, angry, sad, and tired from conflict.
- Violence is not an acceptable way to resolve conflict.
- Resolving conflict brings healing.
- Resolving conflict requires discipline.
- Resolving conflict is a form of peacemaking that involves prayer, listening and repeating back, reducing, and compromising.
- You can't resolve all conflict.

2. Use the following example to work through the skill steps for Resolving Conflict.

Your teen is asked to a party, but his or her two close friends aren't invited. They are angry about it. Your teen asks the host if these two friends can come, but the host says, "There are too many people already." Your teen shares the host's reason with the two friends, but they think the host is making excuses. Your teen also tells the two friends that he or she is still going to the party. For the next three days, your teen's two friends ignore your teen. At this point, your teen shares the situation with you. The party is in two days.

Chapter 6

Forecasting

Goal Setting

Keeping Promises

Identifying Consequences

Choosing Good Friends

Making Changes

Reverencing the Ordinary

Sometimes we don't anticipate the results,
costs, or tasks involved in the decisions
we make. These forecasting skills affect the
vertical, horizontal, and internal dimensions
of our spirituality by helping us think through
important decisions before making them.

Goal Setting

Teach me good judgment and knowledge,
for I believe in your commandments.

Psalm 119:66

Introducing the Skill

Most of the time when teaching adolescents about goal setting, it is best to think in terms of three types of goals—immediate, short-term, and long-term. But within each of those categories, there are different kinds of goals. Some goals focus on what adolescents want for their social life, such as school achievement, athletics, and friendships. Some goals focus on what they want for their emotional life, such as expressing affection, controlling anger, and reducing stress. And some goals focus on their spiritual life, such as how to improve their relationship with God, how to make sense of the mystery and meaning in life, and what it means to live as a disciple of Jesus.

Circle those statements that, in your opinion, best describe your teen's goals.

1. Most of my teen's goals are   *social*   *emotional*   *spiritual*
2. Most of my teen's goals are   *too easy*   *realistic*   *too difficult*

When it comes to my teen's goal setting, I wish

Here's how to help your teen improve his or her social, emotional, and religious goal setting. First, prompt him or her to ask, "*Who* can help me?" God expects us to live in community and rely on others. Encourage your teen to ask a trusted adult or peer to brainstorm ideas with him or her. Second, prompt your teen to ask, "*What* will it demand of me?" Most adolescents can underestimate the challenges involved and the resources needed to reach their social, emotional, and religious goals. Third, prompt your teen to ask, "*Why* should I pursue this?" This question helps young people discover their true motives and determine how much or how little this goal will benefit others as well as themselves. This question allows for an honest check on the quality and integrity of one's motivation.

Which of these questions do you think your teen needs to ask or to think about more often in his or her practice of goal setting? (Circle one)

Who can help me?

What will it demand of me?

Why should I pursue this?

For Yourself

1. Can you identify what kind of goal(s) is/are reflected in each of the different commandments? Use So, E, or Sp to signify whether you think the commandment has a social, emotional, or spiritual goal. Indicate all that you think apply.

_____ I am the Lord your God. You shall not have strange gods before me.

_____ You shall not take the name of the Lord your God in vain.

_____ Remember to keep holy the Lord's day.

_____ Honor your father and your mother.

_____ You shall not kill.

_____ You shall not commit adultery.

_____ You shall not steal.

_____ You shall not bear false witness against your neighbor.

_____ You shall not covet your neighbor's wife.

_____ You shall not covet your neighbor's goods.

2. Which of the commandments affects you the most?

3. Now take a moment to write down two of your goals:

4. Practice goal setting by asking these four questions about your goals:

What kinds of goals are they?

Who can help me with each goal?

What will the goals demand of me?

Why should I pursue these goals?

Using the Skill

1. The question, "What kind of goal is it?" is helpful. In order to help your teen fully develop his or her spirituality, foster goals that are social, emotional, and spiritual in nature.

   Catholicism is rich in its ability to help your teen with his or her religious goals. Our faith overflows with symbols, rituals, colors, gestures, seasons, holy days, mystery, story, beliefs, and history. Be confident in the power of participation. Experience the many aspects of Catholicism with your teen as an intentional means of enriching the religious dimension of his or her spirituality.

   There are times when all adolescents seem too tired to set any social, emotional, or spiritual goals. That's normal. However, some adolescents seem adrift, usually failing to set any goals that capture their imagination or passion. These youth need our assistance. Offer a kind of solidarity with this young person through casual conversation and by spending time doing things together. Eventually you will be more comfortable discussing important issues that can lead directly to discussions of goal setting. But initially it is more important to meet your adolescent's basic needs of positive interaction, friendship, and acceptance.

2. Adolescents tend to be unrealistic when you ask, "Who can help you?" Your teen will usually say, "No one," or "I can do it myself." He or she might also name resource people who lack what it *really* takes to help your teen succeed.

3. Young adolescents often underestimate the cost of goals, so be persistent in asking, "What does this goal demand of you?" Help your teen identify the different layers within the answer, such as time, money, talent, elimination of other goals, and special instruction.

4. The question, "Why are you pursuing this?" is the most important one of all. This question will open doorways to all sorts of other conversations. This is the question that will reveal the *quality* of your teen's goals, the true values your teen holds, and that about which your teen is most passionate.

Passion is the gift many adolescents can teach the rest of us. Whatever you do in helping your adolescent with goal setting, do not kill the passion that fuels his or her goal. Instead, balance your teen's passion with principles. Passion coupled with principles gives birth to compassion. Passion extinguished gives birth to cynicism and apathy.

Keeping Promises

> *"Let your word be 'Yes, Yes' or 'No, No'; anything more than this comes from the evil one."*
>
> Matthew 5:37

Introducing the Skill

All of us want our children to keep their promises. We want them to know that they can be only as good as their word. Promises are matters of character and call for a certain spiritual discipline. Consider placing the following message on your refrigerator: "Every promise you make will show what kind of person you really are."

A young college basketball player left school after his sophomore year to turn pro. While playing for the NBA, he took correspondence courses during the season and attended summer school during the off-season. Three years later he earned his degree. He went to his graduation ceremony in the afternoon and flew back in time to play for his team that evening. That night the team allowed any fan who came to the game with a college ID to get in for only $10. When reporters asked the player for a comment, he replied that he completed college because he wanted to keep his promise to graduate that he made to his mother.

Young adolescents sometimes struggle with impulsiveness. Because of that, they don't always practice forecasting when it comes to making promises. As a result, they make promises they can't keep, promises they shouldn't keep, and promises they have no intention of keeping. Today keeping promises can be as dangerous and unhealthy as breaking them. The stakes are higher, and the consequences can be permanent.

When it comes to helping your teen develop the skill of Keeping Promises, offer these "Dos" and "Don'ts":

DO

- Consider the motive behind the promise—both *your* motive and the motive of the person asking you for a promise. Is the motive a noble one?
- Forecast the cost of the promise *before* making it.
- Tell people that you are under the obligation of a promise. When keeping a promise conflicts with someone or something else, say so. Your friends will understand. You will gain the respect of your friends for staying faithful to a promise made.
- Sacrifice. In order to maintain integrity, keep your word, and fulfill a promise, you will have to give up things, such as being part of certain conversations and going certain places with certain people.
- Talk to an adult if you struggle with making or keeping a promise.

DON'T

- Make promises quickly or automatically. Most of the time it's not necessary. Your *yes* or your *no* should be good enough. (See Jesus' advice from *Matthew 5:37* at the beginning of this skill. Why would Jesus make it a point to include this topic among his teachings? Because it's that important!) Most of the time it is not necessary to hurry a decision. By taking your time to make an informed choice, you won't have to back down from your promise because of poor planning.
- Make promises lightly. Every promise brings responsibility.
- Keep a promise if someone is being hurt or endangered by it.
- Keep a promise that makes you feel uncomfortable or worried. Tell a trusted adult.
- Do something immoral in order to keep a promise.

For Yourself

1. Rate yourself on Keeping Promises by placing a *T* for True or an *F* for False before the following statements.

_____ I make promises only if I know I can keep them.

_____ I make too many promises.

_____ No one asks me to make promises anymore.

_____ I hold my kids accountable for the promises they make.

_____ Keeping promises is a personal priority for me.

_____ I like it when people ask me to keep a promise.

_____ People know that I keep promises.

2. Write a word, initial, or symbol that represents

a time when you made a significant sacrifice in order to keep a noble promise.

a time when you broke a promise and you still regret it.

a time when someone pressured you to keep a promise. Later, you regretted keeping it.

a promise you made to God that you still want to honor or return to.

a promise you still have to keep.

What spiritual strength do you need most when it comes to keeping promises?

Using the Skill

1. Discuss with your teen the "Dos" and "Dont's" of Keeping Promises in the following situations:

Your teen is asked by a friend of the other gender to be his or her date at a school dance.

Your teen is invited to a party at his or her friend's house next weekend. Your teen has promised not to tell anyone that the parents of the host will be out of town and that the host's brother who is a high school junior will be in charge. Your teen has also heard that alcohol will be available at the party.

Your teen is asked to promise not to tell anyone that four friends have stolen a copy of next week's math test.

Your teen wants to promise to give up TV for Lent.

Your teen asks what you would do if a person has asked you to promise not to tell anyone that she was depressed all the time, "crying a lot at night and stuff."

Your teen wants to borrow $100 for the class trip to Washington, D.C., with a promise to pay you back within a month.

2. What are some of your teen's strengths and weaknesses when it comes to Keeping Promises? Share your opinion with him or her. About which do you agree? About which do you disagree?

Strengths   **Weaknesses**

Identifying Consequences

"Everyone then who hears these words of mine and acts on them will be like a wise man who built his house on rock. The rain fell, the floods came, and the winds blew and beat on that house, but it did not fall, because it had been founded on rock."

Matthew 7:24–25

Introducing the Skill

If there is one area of grave concern for parents, it's helping their children identify consequences. It is difficult for adolescents to forecast the consequences of their words, thoughts, and actions. Can we help them become even a little more skilled at identifying consequences of the decisions they make regarding peers, purchases, puberty, playing, and praying? Sometimes the consequences amount to inconveniences in time, money, or effort. But sometimes the consequences have serious moral costs. And there are the complications that come when adolescents act with good intentions—which seems to make forecasting consequences a bit more irrelevant.

There are countless ways to help your teen improve the skill of Identifying Consequences. One way is by using the mnemonic device ROCKS.

R*elationships:* How will your action affect your relationship with self, God, and others?

O*pportunities:* How will this action give you opportunities to express what is in your mind and heart?

C*apabilities:* Do you have the capability to accomplish the task or handle the consequences? (This is similar to a step in the skill of Goal Setting)

K*nowledge:* What knowledge do you need to accomplish the task? Where can you find the advice or information needed? How can you use what you already know?

S*tumbling blocks:* What obstacles or challenges are you likely to encounter, and how will you deal with those?

Now practice using ROCKS on one of the following situations.
Your teen tells a racist joke at school.

Your teen announces that he or she wants to learn to play a musical instrument.

For Yourself

1. Which of the consequences in ROCKS are most important to you?

> *Relationships*   *Opportunities*   *Capabilities*
>
> *Knowledge*   *Stumbling blocks*

2. Where are you having the most success in making choices by identifying consequences?

> *Work*   *Counseling friends*
>
> *Favorite hobby*   *Family dynamics*
>
> *Your teen's behavior*   *Living your faith*

3. Who or what has been most helpful to you when it comes to identifying consequences?

4. Now try using ROCKS to forecast the consequences of a real situation that you are facing.

Name the situation.

How will your choice affect your relationships?

What opportunities will this choice provide you?

Which of your capabilities must you draw upon, or will be developed by your choice?

What knowledge do you need, and how will others react when they know of your choice?

What stumbling blocks are you going to encounter before and after this choice? How will you deal with these?

Using the Skill

1. In addition to using ROCKS as a means of helping your teen with the skill of Identifying Consequences, you can also use the Eight Developmental Needs of Adolescents (EDNA) that were described in Chapter 1—physical activity, self-definition, competence and achievement, religious experience, creative expression, positive interaction with peers and adults, meaningful participation, structure and limits. To do so, use the chart below. Simply list in the space provided any of the EDNA that are met (or hurt, as the case may be) in each of the following situations.

- Your teen signs up for a service project with the parish youth group.
- Your teen comes home from an outing with a hickey on his or her neck.
- Your teen wants to go to Mass on Saturday evening with friends instead of going with you on Sunday morning.
- Your teen comes home on time from an outing, but you smell alcohol on his or her breath.
- You discover from your latest phone bill that your teen has called a phone sex number twice.

Action	Needs Met	Needs Hurt
Service project		
Hickey		
Mass with friends		
Alcohol		
Calling phone sex numbers		

Talk through each of the examples with your teen. Discuss possible consequences with him or her.

Choosing Good Friends

Faithful friends are a sturdy shelter:
*   whoever finds one has found a treasure.*
Faithful friends are beyond price;
*   no amount can balance their worth.*
Faithful friends are life-saving medicine;
*   and those who fear the Lord will find them.*
Those who fear the Lord direct their friendship aright,
*   for as they are, so are their neighbors also.*

Sirach 6:14–17

Introducing the Skill

All of us need friends. But for young adolescents, friendships seem to matter more than anything else. As they sort through their own personalities and emotions, adolescents interchange friends at a rapid pace. But throughout this uncertainty young adolescents still look for one or two trustworthy and compatible friends.

The key to coaching your teen in the skill of Choosing Good Friends lies in making the distinction between a friend who is loyal and a friend who is both loyal and good.

Write the initials of one of your teen's loyal friends about whom you have concerns.

Write the initials of one of your teen's friends who seems to be a good person.

Choosing good friends—that is, friends who are both loyal and good—is a matter of recognizing goodness in peers and investing in a relationship with those persons. By "goodness" we are referring to such virtues as kindness, patience, gentleness, self-control, joy, generosity, love, peace, and faithfulness. The Bible calls these the fruit of the Spirit. (See *Galatians 5:22–23.*)

The skill of Choosing Good Friends calls for a great deal of prudence and fortitude.

Does your teen seem to invest more time with loyal friends or friends who are both loyal and good?

What criteria do you think your teen uses in choosing friends?

On a scale of 1–5 (1 being poor, 5 being excellent), how would you rate your teen's ability to choose friends who are good?

For Yourself

1. List the first name or initials of the following friends:

   Long-time friend I still have:

   Friend I wish I still had:

   Good friend who is much younger:

   Good friend who is much older:

   Good friend of the same gender:

   Good friend of the other gender:

   Good friend living out of state:

   Good friend I see only during certain seasons, events, or activities:

2. Name one or two fruits of the Spirit you recognize in some of these friends.

3. What fruits of the Spirit do you appreciate the most in friends who are good?

4. What fruits of the Spirit would your friends say they see in you?

5. The first page of this skill contains a proverb on friendship from the Book of Sirach. Write one or two proverbs of your own about some aspect of Choosing Good Friends.

Using the Skill

1. Sometimes you may have to coach your teen on how to terminate an unhealthy friendship. Keep in mind that your teen's physical safety, mental health, and spiritual well-being are more important than keeping an overly dependent friend happy, hurting someone's feelings, or getting rejected by a member of a peer group. Refer to related skills in this book, such as Dealing with Anxiety, Staying Hopeful, Goal Setting, and Identifying Consequences, when coaching your teen through the process of terminating unhealthy friendships.

2. Friendships are never as simple and neat as we like to think. Few friendships are perfect. Here's a chance to practice coaching your teen with those complex and messy friendships that come along from time to time.

While producing a video program on the value of character, a group of high school students were asked, "Is it important that a good friend be a person of character?" With cameras rolling, one of them said, "Not really. My best friend is untruthful. I don't believe a word he tells me. He never tells the complete truth. He never admits to anything he does wrong. But he's my best friend because he is loyal. He will help me out every time I need him. My dad died when I was young, and my friend has stuck by me closer than a brother."

What important insight does this give you about adolescent friendship?

What question would you have for this young person if he or she were your child?

What question(s) about friendship do you want to ask your teen?

3. Share with your teen the qualities you look for in a friend and some of your experiences of friendship. Ask your teen to do the same.

Making Changes

We know that all things work together for good for those who love God, who are called according to his purpose.

Romans 8:28

Introducing the Skill

Growth brings change. As we grow, our mental abilities, verbal skills, and physical strength increase. We can't help it; it's the way we were created. Each change brings a bit of excitement, fear, and doubt, and occasionally anger and sadness.

As a parent or guardian, you will see your young person change in ways that will make you smile, growing into young adulthood with the values and characteristics you have worked so hard to instill. But you will also feel a certain sense of loss as he or she grows away from some of the tenderness, innocence, and loyalty of childhood.

No one experiences more changes in such a short amount of time than your teen and his or her peers. Adolescence is all about change. Some resist change, while others force change prematurely. And many young people haven't been taught what to keep in mind when making changes.

How has your teen changed in a way that makes you sad?

How has your teen changed in a way that makes you happy?

What changes have been hardest for your teen to handle?

Make a list for your teen of five things to keep in mind when making changes.

Things to Keep in Mind When Making Changes

1.

2.

3.

4.

5.

For Yourself

How do you approach Making Changes?

1. Check off all of the following that are true about you.

○ I think change makes things interesting.

○ Change is easy for me.

○ I hate change.

○ I deliberately make changes often.

○ If I need to make a change, I think long and hard about what's involved.

○ I just let change happen, instead of making change.

○ I've had good experiences with making changes.

○ I've experienced a lot of tough changes.

2. Over which one or two of the following have you recently made the most significant change? (Circle your choices.)

My looks	My emotions
My perspective on things	My friendships
My family life	My work
My lifestyle	How I use my time
My reading habits	My TV viewing habits
My eating habits	My spiritual life
My health	My spending habits
My involvement in community service	Other:

3. Identify an important change you must make in the near future. Then outline what you will need to keep in mind in making this change.

4. If God asked you to consider making a change in your spiritual life, what do you think that would be? What would be the toughest thing about making that change?

Using the Skill

1. Discuss with your teen the changes that will happen within the family in each of the following situations and what the family can do to help make the change go smoothly.

   - Your parents (their grandparents) have retired and are moving away.
   - Due to a layoff, the family income will be reduced for an indeterminate time.

2. Keep in mind the skill of Making Changes as you discuss with your teen changes that may occur for him or her by the end of high school. Make some notes in the space provided about each topic.

   Friendships

   Sports and other activities

   Academic interests

   Physical appearance

   Spiritual growth

   Family ties

   Your relationship

   Work

   Finances

Reverencing the Ordinary

> *[T]he fruit of the Spirit is love, joy, peace, patience, kindness, generosity, faithfulness, gentleness, and self-control.*
>
> Galatians 5:22–23

Introducing the Skill

God is everywhere. We hear that all the time. We know that God can often be found in the religious elements of our culture, and so we hold our holy days, rituals, and prayers as sacred.

But since God is everywhere, **the present is sacred and the ordinary is holy.** Wouldn't your teen's spirituality be continually nurtured and enhanced if he or she learned to reverence the ordinary? Reverencing the Ordinary is a spiritual skill that involves enjoying the goodness in something and acknowledging it. This is different from simply recognizing goodness. You can recognize a fruit by its appearance, but it is a much richer experience to recognize a fruit by its taste. "Tasting" the fruit brings the enjoyment of taking it inside.

The spiritual skill of Reverencing the Ordinary involves "tasting" any of the real human qualities of goodness described in *Galatians 5* (above) and letting God know that you enjoyed it. Here's an example illustrating the skill of Reverencing the Ordinary:

A young man told an adult interviewer, "I was in the front row at this really awesome concert a month ago, and you could feel all the energy, excitement, and unity from all the people packed together just before the band came out. I couldn't believe where I was, standing right there by the stage and feeling connected to all these strangers! I looked around at all the excited people, and I don't know, I just started praying to myself right there, thanking God for everything!"

Which fruit of the Spirit did this young person "taste"?

How does this illustrate the difference between "tasting" and recognizing?

For Yourself

1. If you were blindfolded, which of these fruits could you recognize by taste if they each came to you in the identical form of a custard? (Circle your responses.)

Banana	Blackberry	Raspberry
Pear	Plum	Mango
Peach	Orange	Tangerine
Apricot	Nectarine	Grapefruit
Strawberry	Apple	Blueberry

2. Which of these human qualities of goodness have you enjoyed from an ordinary event, conversation, action, observation, song, movie, or TV show? (Circle your responses.)

Love	Joy	Peace
Patience	Kindness	Generosity
Faithfulness	Gentleness	Self-control

3. *Every week while shopping at the supermarket, you notice the same woman behind the Customer Service desk. Each time, you see angry and rude people standing in the line, waiting to complain about items they want to return. The woman never gets riled or disturbed by people's short, rough, and often disrespectful interactions. Today, as you wait to return something, you notice that she stops what she's doing and steps from behind the desk to greet her daughter and kiss her grandson who are in the store buying their groceries.*

Practice Reverencing the Ordinary now by identifying the fruit of the Spirit you have tasted and letting God know how much you enjoyed it.

4. Recall one of your most recent experiences of Reverencing the Ordinary. Jot down a word or sketch a symbol that represents that experience. Also name which fruit of the Spirit you tasted.

Using the Skill

1. Remember the two steps to Reverencing the Ordinary: "tasting" goodness of some kind and letting God know how much you enjoyed it. Use the steps often in the presence of your teen.

2. One of the best things you can do to reinforce this skill with your teen is to point out the human qualities of goodness—or fruits of the Spirit—when you see them. You can practice this by identifying how the different fruits of the Spirit are shared in the following situations.

While in the gym, Caitlin saw that a fight was about to start, so she went over and calmed everyone down.

When José noticed that James had forgotten his lunch and didn't have any money, he gave James half his sandwich.

Even though you were nearly an hour late picking up your teen after school, he or she sat there patiently reading a book.

Your teen danced to your car with his or her latest report card and jumped in with a big smile.

Your teen wants to get on the Internet and check e-mail, but has decided to finish his or her homework first.

3. Take a moment to identify and give thanks for the fruits of the Spirit you have enjoyed in your teen recently. Point these out to him or her.

4. Periodically share with your teen an experience from your day in which you reverence the ordinary. Ask your teen to share a similar experience from his or her day.

Chapter 7

A
Practicing
Catholic

Living Our Catholic Beliefs

Putting Our Faith In Action

Assessing Practices: Living My Faith

"What good is it, my brothers and sisters, if you say you have faith but do not have works...just as the body without the spirit is dead, so faith without works is also dead."

James 2:14, 26

As children it is easy to envision faith as a Sunday event—Sunday is the day to believe. We go to Mass and stand during which we recite the Creed, *"I believe in God, the Father Almighty...."* Monday arrives, and we engage in living the rest of our "real" life. These acts can remain two separate endeavors, until one day we realize that faith is not about "believing" on Sunday and "living" the rest of the week— faith is about *living our beliefs* every day and in every way. Suddenly, all the religion classes our parents sent us to start to make sense and serve a purpose: We *learn* about our faith so we can better *live* our faith through our daily choices and interactions with others. This is the connection between faith and works. This is putting "Sunday faith" into everyday life. Practicing our faith involves more than reciting the words of the Creed. We need to understand *what* the words mean, *why* they matter, and *how* they affect the choices we make in daily life.

Putting Our Faith In Action

Being a Catholic involves not only *what* we believe (our creed), but *who* we are (our values) and *how* we act (our practices). Our lifestyle is the integration and expression of our identity—our beliefs, values, and practices. The skills in this book provide practical tools for putting our beliefs into practice. They are meant to assist us, and the teens we know, in practicing our faith every day.

The image of "practicing" our faith is a comforting one. Often as teens we practiced the piano, dance, or any of a variety of sports. Although the focus of practicing was different, the function was the same. And we soon discovered practicing was a never-ending activity—no matter how much we practiced one week, we always had something more to learn and practice the next week. With each new lesson or skill came improved performance, never perfect, but always stronger.

Practicing meant being *intentional* about learning and doing the things that would make us a stronger player. Practicing strengthened us in three ways: confidence, commitment, and competence. It helped us become more ready, willing, and able to "be at our best" all the time. We may have skipped practicing or simply "put in time" without exerting any real effort, and of course, our abilities would wane. But, if we reengaged in practicing with sincere effort, we usually regained our skills and abilities, and often reignited our passion for the activity as well.

Similarly, practicing our faith helps us to become more confident, committed, competent Catholics. Catholic practices encourage us to "be at our best" as children of God. Our faith enables us to be ready, willing, and able disciples of Jesus Christ in the world. We may lapse in our practicing now and then, or simply "put in time" some weeks. However, on any given day, we can actively reengage in the practices to regain our strength and rekindle our passion for our faith. The Gifts and Fruits of the Holy Spirit we learned about in preparing for Confirmation truly are present and available for our use every day, but we have to open them—or maybe take them out of storage first!

So what does it mean to "be Catholic" and live a Catholic Christian lifestyle in today's world? What are the everyday practices that make us Catholic? How can we keep our faith truly alive, not only in our parish community, but also in our home, on the ball field, in the community, and even in our mini-van?

Gather a random group of Catholics and ask them to describe what it means to "be Catholic" and how they practice their faith. You will likely hear very diverse responses, but with some similar underling themes. One of the gifts of Catholicism is its wide range of spirituality and expressions of a common faith, both locally and globally. The Catholic Church honors and embraces the diversity of cultural faith customs around the world. There are truly many parts to the one Body of Christ. Although we profess the same Creed, each Catholic may emphasize a particular way to express his or her faith, hold a deeper passion for a particular ministry of the Church, or treasure a particular form of prayer. Yet, the basic practices of being Catholic are truly universal.

Practicing Catholics Intentionally...

† Honor the Gift and Goodness of All Life

Catholics respect life in all its forms as created by God. We strive to protect and promote life, and appreciate the diversity of life expressed through other faiths and cultures.

† Take Time to Be with God

Catholics spend intentional time with God through personal prayer, praying with others, and celebrating the sacraments as a source of spiritual strength, especially by participating in the Eucharist.

† Take Time to Be with the People of God

Catholics participate in the life and mission of the Church as active members of a parish, offering time, talent, and treasure in service to God through the ministries of the faith community. We need and value the strength, support, comfort, and challenge that a faith community can provide.

† Seek and See God in the Ordinary

Catholics strive to both see and be God's presence in daily life. We recognize the potential holiness of ordinary moments: the power of a kind word, the laughter of children, an understanding smile, or helpful gesture. We call on the Spirit to be with us and to act through us.

† Live a Forgiving Life

Catholics recognize and appreciate the generous mercy, unconditional love, and unending forgiveness of God. We look to the example of Christ who shared God's mercy with those around him. We strive to accept imperfections, acknowledge our mistakes, forgive ourselves and others, value reconciliation, and to believe in the power of change.

† Live a Life for Giving

Catholics adopt justice and service as a consistent attitude and lifestyle. We see life as a blessing from God, and practice good stewardship by sharing our blessings: offering hospitality and care to those in need, acting charitably toward others, and working for justice in society as disciples of Jesus Christ.

† Live a Lifelong Spiritual Journey

Catholics strive to nurture a personal spirituality, and develop sensitivity to God's call and the work of the Spirit throughout our lifetimes. We strive to make spiritual sense out of the many turns, setbacks, and discoveries along the pathway of life.

† Embody Catholic Tradition

Catholics appreciate the long and strong practices of the Church, handed down through many generations. We turn to Scripture, Catholic Tradition and Church teaching as sources for nurturing our faith, forming our conscience, and guiding our moral choices.

Assessing Practices: Living My Faith

As you reflect on the general practices of being Catholic, consider these questions:

1. *How are these practices reflected in my own life?*

2. *How does my teen practice his or her faith?*

3. *How does my family practice our faith together?*

4. *How might the skills in this book help me in practicing my faith?*

You can use this reflection process individually and as a family.

- Complete this reflection for yourself, ask your teen to complete it, and together consider how you are practicing the faith as a family. Encourage your teen to voice suggestions.
- Identify one or two things that you want to do individually and as a family to "practice" your faith more intentionally.
- Consider what skills in this book might expand or enhance your ability to both learn about and live your faith each week.
- In a few weeks or months, reassess the practices again and discuss what impact they had on you, your teen and the family.

Catholic Practices	By me	By my teen	As a family
Honor the Gift and Goodness of All Life			
Take Time to Be with God			
Take Time to Be with the People of God			
Seek and See God in the Ordinary			
Live a Forgiving Life			
Live a Life For Giving			
Live a Lifelong Spiritual Journey			
Embody Catholic Tradition			

Reflection

Use these reflection questions in three ways:
- privately for your own reflection
- give them to your teen for his or her reflection
- use them as a focus for conversation between you and your teen

1. In your own words, what does it mean to you to "be Catholic?"

Being Catholic means....

2. What characteristics, beliefs, customs, or practices of the Catholic faith are you most drawn toward in your faith?

What I'm most drawn to about the Catholic faith is...

3. What is that hardest thing about being a practicing Catholic in the world today?

For me, the hardest thing about practicing my faith is...

4. List three of the most primary beliefs you hold as a Catholic:

I believe...

I believe...

I believe...

5. Now consider how you practice those beliefs in your daily choices. How do your beliefs shape your attitude and views, your decisions, and your interactions with other people?

Because I believe   , I strive to...

Because I believe   , I strive to...

Because I believe   , I strive to...

6. If someone visited your home, how would they know you were Catholic? What signs, symbols, or activities would they see that communicate your faith?

7. Describe some of the practical ways you practice your faith throughout the week:

privately by myself...

at home with family....

with my friends....

with people I meet, but don't know...

at work or school...

at worship and in the parish...

in the broader community...

Reminders

In addition to the skills outlined in this book, the following "Reminders" might also contribute to the ongoing conversations you and your teen will have about being Catholic.

Thank you for working through this book. We hope you have found some helpful ways to nurture the spirituality of your teen, and continue to grow in practicing your faith as a family.

Nicene Creed

We believe in one God,
 the Father, the Almighty,
 maker of heaven and earth,
 of all that is seen and unseen.
We believe in one Lord, Jesus Christ,
 the only Son of God,
 eternally begotten of the Father,
 God from God, Light from Light,
 true God from true God,
 begotten, not made, one in Being with the Father.
 Through him all things were made.
 For us men and for our salvation
 he came down from heaven:
 by the power of the Holy Spirit he was born of the Virgin Mary, and
 became man.
 For our sake he was crucified under Pontius Pilate;
 he suffered, died, and was buried.
 On the third day he rose again
 in fulfillment of the Scriptures;
 he ascended into heaven
 and is seated at the right hand of the Father.
 He will come again in glory to judge the living and the dead,
 and his kingdom will have no end.
We believe in the Holy Spirit, the Lord, the giver of life,
 who proceeds from the Father and the Son.
 With the Father and the Son he is worshiped and glorified.
 He has spoken through the Prophets.
We believe in one holy catholic and apostolic Church.
We acknowledge one baptism for the forgiveness of sins.

We look for the resurrection of the dead,
    and the life of the world to come.
    Amen.

Precepts of the Church

1. Take part in the Mass on Sundays and holy days. Keep these days holy and avoid unnecessary work.
2. Celebrate the Sacrament of Reconciliation at least once a year if there is serious sin.
3. Receive Holy Communion at least once a year during Easter time.
4. Fast and abstain on days of penance.
5. Give your time, gifts, and money to support the Church.

The Ten Commandments

1. I am the Lord your God. You shall not have strange god's before me.
2. You shall not take the name of the Lord your God in vain.
3. Remember to keep holy the Lord's day.
4. Honor your father and your mother.
5. You shall not kill.
6. You shall not commit adultery.
7. You shall not steal.
8. You shall not bear false witness against your neighbor.
9. You shall not covet your neighbor's wife.
10. You shall not covet your neighbor's goods.

The Beatitudes

Blessed are the poor in spirit, for theirs is the kingdom of heaven.
Blessed are they who mourn, for they will be comforted.
Blessed are the meek, for they will inherit the land.
Blessed are they who hunger and thirst for righteousness,
    for they will be satisfied.
Blessed are the merciful, for they will be shown mercy.
Blessed are the clean of heart, for they will see God.
Blessed are the peacemakers, for they will be called children of God.
Blessed are they who are persecuted for the sake of righteousness,
    for theirs is the kingdom of heaven.

Gifts of the Holy Spirit

Wisdom
Understanding
Right judgment (Counsel)
Courage (Fortitude)

Knowledge
Reverence (Piety)
Wonder and awe (Fear of the Lord)

Fruits of the Spirit

Charity	Generosity
Joy	Gentleness
Peace	Faithfulness

Kindness	Patience
Goodness	Modesty
Self-control	Chastity

Works of Mercy

Corporal (for the body)
Feed the hungry.
Give drink to the thirsty.
Clothe the naked.
Shelter the homeless.
Visit the sick.
Visit the imprisoned.
Bury the dead.
Comfort the sorrowful.

Spiritual (for the spirit)
Warn the sinner.
Teach the ignorant.
Counsel the doubtful.
Comfort the sorrowful.
Bear wrongs patiently.
Forgive injuries.
Pray for the living and the dead.